Duck

An

Outer

Banks

Village

For my Real Friend
 Marleanie —
Thank you for taking
care of my children and
always being a real friend.
          Love,
          Deborah

JOHN F. BLAIR,

PUBLISHER

Winston-Salem, North Carolina

Duck

An
Outer Banks
Village

Judith D. Mercier

Published by John F. Blair, Publisher

*The paper in this book meets the guidelines
for permanence and durability of the
Committee on Production Guidelines for
Book Longevity of the Council on Library Resources.*

Library of Congress Cataloging-in-Publication Data

Mercier, Judith D.
Duck: an Outer Banks village / Judith D. Mercier.
p.   cm.
Includes index.
ISBN 0-89587-236-6 (alk. paper)
1. Duck (N.C.)—History. 2. Duck (N.C.)—Biography.
I. Title: Outer Banks village. II. Title.
F264.D83 M47 2001
975.6'175—dc21

2001018491

Design by Debra Long Hampton

To Mary, who fills me with hope;
to May and Charlie, who showered me with goodness;
and to Peter and Petey, who bring me laughter and love

Contents

Prologue   ix

I Wind and Water   3

II The Duck Man   35

III Outsiders   65

IV Searching for Hargraves Beach   101

V Lessons of a Duck Hunter   149

VI Duck Road   191

VII Dennis and Other Menaces   235

Epilogue   247
Acknowledgments   255
Index   257

Prologue

A pinch of earth separates the Atlantic Ocean from the Currituck Sound. Generations ago, a meager band of seafarers, fishermen, and duck hunters settled this area of North Banks land. They and their families built a small community, a neighborhood sheltered by the oaks and pines growing atop the sand hills. Today, thousands of summer tourists visit the same place, a bantam village they know as Duck.

Duck constitutes barely 2 percent of the land area of North Carolina's Outer Banks. Virtually hidden until the early 1980s, the village and its inhabitants enjoyed several centuries of solitude and anonymity. Only within the past two decades have eager developers transformed Duck into the last summer boom town in Dare County. Now, rental properties far outstrip the duck blinds that once freckled the Currituck, and realtors and retailers far outnumber the duck hunters and fishermen who, with their wives and children, subsisted on hope, self-reliance, and the area's natural bounty.

I began visiting Duck in 1989. Already, it had garnered media attention. Articles in Northern newspapers and national travel magazines declared its beauty and simple charm. Initially, I considered Duck a sort of hallowed playground. Despite the throngs of tourists and the crush of traffic, Duck's secluded beaches provided a chrism for the body. Its sound-side marsh seemed a balm for the mind. In Duck, I could strip off every layer of mainland life, start over as callow as a foundling, think myself and the world around me unspoiled and unblemished.

Along Duck's oceanfront, I have watched the sun rise, heard the words of Genesis as if spoken by the Creator himself, the spirit of God hovering over the water. I have been coddled and admonished by Duck's parental forces: the maternal sea, her saline womb a deep, mysterious comfort, her spray a fond perfume, her slap as powerful as her splendor; the paternal wind, drying and directing, soothing or surly, ever watchful, ever present, the brawn and master, the air of pleasure and authority.

Eventually, the village proved to be more than a

carefully planned Eden built on sand. Maybe it was a mixture of devotion and gratitude that drew me to these narratives about Duck. Perhaps it was innocent curiosity that motivated my early explorations. Surely, this project was undertaken as a selfish act. It offered dozens of good reasons why I should return to Duck, visit the village in every season, study it in sunshine and rain, know its temperate westerly breezes as well as its frigid northeasterly gusts, investigate its family graveyards and curious street names.

Over the course of three years, I spent a few months' worth of lazy days talking to village natives and newcomers and a few weeks' worth of sleepless nights menaced by howling winds and rising tides. During that time, I grew to appreciate Duck in all its moods and mutations and to admire the people, both living and dead, who have had a stake in it. Beneath the village's modern finery, there's another Duck, one that existed years ago, a place rough and untamed.

The following accounts are fed by two opposing powers, those of nature and man. For the fate of Duck is continually altered by whims and wills, some human, some not. This collection includes voices from the village's past and present and whispers of its future—both destinies previously met and those yet to be realized.

Without any grandiose ancestry, Duck remains a place worth knowing. Its people are worth meeting, its heritage worth guarding. Stories are what bolster the spine of this coastal community, an old village bent but not yet broken. For that reason alone, these are stories worth telling.

꩜ ꩜ ꩜ ꩜ ꩜ ꩜ ꩜ ꩜

Duck

An
Outer
Banks
Village

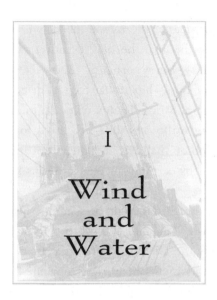

I

Wind
and
Water

It's a stiff day. Every board cracks brittle as bone beneath my feet. I'm standing alone on the wooden walkway that connects the Duck Waterfront Shops, where the village meets the Currituck Sound.

In summer, when this wood is supple and these planks a promenade, I come here at dusk, one pilgrim among the many sated by days of whitecaps and white-hot sand. Our vacations almost spent, we tourists perform twilight rituals: drifting in and out of the stores, pressing ourselves between racks of hand-painted T-shirts and rows of rubber rafts, leaving our fingerprints on the blown-glass pelicans and the lacquered sand dollars, picking through the plastic souvenirs. We wear stained smiles—berry sorbet or cherry ice still red and sweet on our lips—buy dollar bags of dried corn from Duck's General Store. Then we line up to cast the kernels over the walkway railing, to listen for the cackle of a few mother mallards and their mottled ducklings as the sky turns carmine and the sun slips low into the water.

Today, the clouds could be winding sheets, the sun a circle of ash. The chill is too bitter to be so close to spring. Only the Currituck offers sanctuary, a place to hide from this incessant northeast wind. It arrived in the dark like the Midnight Express, a rushing howl that rousted me from sleep. For now, the line of stores will make a good bulwark between us, though only a fool would believe she could escape this wind for long.

It's off-season, morning, almost everything closed, the shops empty, the village hollowed out and simple, the way I imagine it used to be. Under the awning of Sunset Ice Cream, midway between the Blue Point Restaurant and North Beach Sailing and Outfitters, I search my coat pockets for gloves but find instead a visitors' guide to coastal North Carolina that a local realtor gave me years ago. On the faded cover, Duck, about an inch below the Virginia line, maybe thirty miles south, looks like a clumsily drawn rectangle, irregular, out of proportion, too skinny for its four-mile length along the northern Outer Banks.

In good weather, Duck looks fleshy, meatier than its widest breadth of a half-mile. Even farther north, where the village narrows, broomstraw rush, yaupon, Spanish bayonet, catbrier, and sweet bay plump up the ranging sand hills that separate the Currituck from the Atlantic. Beach morning glory and seaside evening primrose dress the dunes in pink trumpets and yellow teacups. Scattered groves grow thick with live oak and loblolly pine, their roots like anchors set in loose soil, their branches a canopy for the sound-side road.

A matronly landscape, Duck feels as safe and sure as a grandmother's lap. Wide dunes, a wooded marsh, the sloping beachfront—everything is cushioned and curved, ample and voluptuous. But these contours are deceptive, merely illusions of permanence and possession. Like anyplace on the Outer Banks, Duck is as fragile as a bird's wing. Wind, whether coming as a northeast gale or a tropical hurricane, can drive the sea to gouge out a hunk of the village, uproot the trees, flatten the sand hills and anything growing on them.

I look to the mainland, Currituck County, where the wind makes less mischief. It may sway in the treetops, comb the grass, show an occasional outburst, but for the most part, it comes and goes without much of a fracas. Just three miles across the sound, in this grainy spit of a village suspended in the Atlantic, the wind broods and schemes. Ordaining the shape of things, it provokes the sea, churns waves, pushes the dunes around. A mad plotter of destinies, this wind proves a fickle companion, cantankerous one day, amiable the next, a ubiquitous force that fractures or fuses, its mutable nature never satisfied until it has hewed the land and the lives of those who come here.

I've read stories about this wind, how it has powered the Atlantic to seize these shores numerous times, washing out tons of sand, then bringing it all back again. Since the sixteenth century, wind and water have carved twenty-two inlets from Carova to Cape Lookout, a 175-mile length of Outer Banks. Six cut through the Currituck Banks alone. A few miles north of here, Caffey's Inlet opened sometime around 1790. Two years before, George Caffey had proudly purchased a hundred acres, then confidently added forty more, before the wind-forced water washed away a wide swath of it. Luckier than some, Caffey recovered much of his investment within ten years. The inlet shoaled, as if the wind had convinced the water that it was time to patch up the land and give most of it back. Even now, Sanderling, the area adjacent to Caffey's Inlet, measures only one-tenth of a mile in width. A veritable finger of sand, it is a constant reminder of this contentious wind and how it conspires with water.

Less than two hundred years ago, the Currituck was brackish. A thirty-five-mile-long estuary, it fed on the last remaining inlet, New Currituck, which, having broken through the North Banks during a heavy storm in the 1730s, lingered for almost a century. Over time, other storms filled in the space between sound and sea with sand, in a process geologists call "natural sedimentation." By 1828, no inlets remained open along the Currituck. The result is this hearty marsh gorged with mud and thriving with *Phragmites australis*, a common reed.

Long before the Currituck was fresh water, when trickles of briny Atlantic still seeped into it, Poteskeet hunters paddled across the sound in boats made from hulled-out trees, maybe docking just beyond this wooden walkway. Back then, when the area teemed with good meat, the Poteskeets depended on what is now Duck and adjacent lands on the North Banks for nourishment. They came first with bows and arrows, later with the guns the white men had traded them for tobacco, copper, or the wampum shells thought to be pearls. Over the marsh and the dunes, the Poteskeets tracked pigs, cows, and goats fattened on salt-meadow hay and cordgrass.

This morning's air, sharp with salt and mist, stings like a shower of Poteskeet arrowheads. A stiff gust shudders a row of stacked kayaks. They flip, then tumble, bump, and bruise the grass, lie askance along the edge of the water. Such a volatile force may have discouraged the Poteskeets from making a permanent home on the North Banks. Indigenous people rarely settled on these barrier islands. The only established tribe, the Croatan Indians, lived farther south, burrowed deep within the woods on Hatteras Island.

Like other native tribes, the Poteskeets respected the power of the wind. They thought of it as they might a great chieftain or warrior, a reckoning master, an invincible spirit. To them, the wind was as palpable as a human heart, as formidable as the will of a god.

The Poteskeets kept a village on the Currituck mainland almost directly across from where I stand. They built their huts—four poles covered with bark and woven rush mats—in a circle north of Powell's Point. They fished in the North River, tended small farms, grew the staples of the early Carolina diet, pagatour (what the white man later called "Indian corn") and openauk (the white potato).

In the summer of 1585, the Poteskeets met white men for the first time. A wave of British explorers reached the coast, then traveled inland under the guise of seeking a surer place to build a new colony, a site protected from the wind. Financed by Sir Walter Raleigh and blessed by their virgin queen, Elizabeth, these explorers followed Philip Amadas and Arthur Barlow, who had already spent a summer surveying the Outer Banks the year before.

The second landing party arrived on an inclement day in late June, coming ashore near Ocracoke. Among them were Ralph Lane, the elected governor, and Thomas Hariot, a scientist and historian. It was Lane's idea to venture north from Hatteras, where the fleet had set anchor. Though he was expected only to supervise the building of a settlement on Roanoke Island, Lane set out toward the Currituck mainland, taking forty men with him. Lane sought the precious metals rumored to be found north of the colonists' intended camp. By early August, he and his company reached Weapomeiok, the Poteskeets' province, where Chief Okisco lived. Though their meeting was unexceptional, Lane's single-minded search for pearls and copper, his deceptive intentions, and his demands that local tribes furnish his men with food and supplies fueled a tempest of mistrust and ill will between the would-be settlers and their native hosts.

A year after meeting Lane and his men, the Poteskeets probably received the disturbing news: the visiting colonists had launched a surprise attack on the main village of the Roanokes. The Poteskeets must have wondered why Lane would ambush this unsuspecting coastal tribe. They also must have pondered what drove Lane's Irish servant, Nugent, to hunt Wingina, a brave Roanoke warrior and noble chief, like an animal. With each report came more apprehension. Every detail of Wingina's beheading seemed to echo the warnings that he had given the Poteskeets and other mainland tribes only months before his death: the white men traveled fast and couldn't be trusted. Eventually, they would bring their destruction across the Currituck.

An especially fierce storm moved over the Outer Banks the day Lane and his men decided to desert the fort on Roanoke Island. Within two days, they boarded a ship and were sailing home to England.

The Poteskeets may have suspected that only the wind could destroy or save them. Bringing peril, it blew pale danger off the ocean and onto their land. Then with the same force, it sent the strangers away, forcing them back across the sea. For a time, the natives could feel safe again.

But another squall is always brewing somewhere in the Atlantic. On the Outer Banks, wind and water fashion the sand each day, every life and story.

❧ ❧ ❧

This morning down at Wee Winks, the only convenience store open in Duck this time of year, the parking lot hums with running pickups. Inside, construction workers crowd around the coffee machine and commiserate about the weather. They breakfast on Slim Jims and corn chips, hold Styrofoam cups close to their chins, let the steam curl over their lips as if to warm their mumbling about the cold. They complain of having to balance themselves on half-built roofs and worry about the thin scaffolding that shimmies on days like this. A few lament their thin socks, their forgotten long johns.

The cashier, a petite blonde with a toothy grin, seems

excited. "How are ya?" she asks the first man in line.

"I'm here and just as happy as I can be," he says, slapping a few dollars on the counter.

"Wind's up," she says.

"Yep."

"Cold out there, isn't it?"

"Damn cold."

"Heard we might get snow," she says.

"Oh yeah, that would be great. We can work in the snow. Probably freeze to death, but we can work in snow."

The workers nurse their cups of coffee. When it's time to face the wind, they move in pairs to the front of the store. They stand on tiptoe, peek over the shelves and through the windows. Sand swirls in low funnels, and broken branches skitter along the asphalt. The men look like paratroopers on a first mission, unsure whether they are ready to jump and who should go first. They size up one another, taking a quick inventory of the others' muscle and courage. Cans of chewing tobacco pass through their hands like communion. Many brace themselves with a burning plug tucked behind their cheek.

"Here I go," one announces. With a tug on his collar, camouflage jacket pulled tight across his chest, he shoulders the door. There's a whoop and a holler, then a bang and a honk, his signal of a safe landing.

The others move in closer, their shoulders hunched,

their heads half hidden under wool caps. We wait for the next volunteer.

"I guess this is it." A second man follows.

Soon, they are all outside, engines revving, tires squealing in the road.

"I feel bad for those guys on days like today," the cashier tells me. "But it's building season. Houses still going up. Gotta get 'em done by summer. It's good-paying work when you can get it."

A wisp of a man flutters into Wee Winks like a village specter. The cashier calls him Joe. He pats a few silver hairs down over a furrowed forehead, then rubs his hands together and taps each foot against the floor. "Gotta get the cold out," he says.

Joe gives updates about the wind. "Gusts already up to sixty." He asks the cashier if she has heard about the snow that might move into Duck from Washington, D.C. "My boy still lives in Arlington," he says. Joe rolls a local paper, the *Coastland Times*, inside a *Washington Post*. "They're expecting at least six inches around the capital." His voice is raspy. Something rattles in his chest. Joe holds up a palm filled with change while the cashier picks out a few quarters and dimes. "Sky looks full of the stuff to me," he says. "Wind's bringing the whole mess in. High tide could flood us."

In some towns, strangers mention the weather for something to say. It makes for an easy, short conversation. In Duck, the subject of weather is almost certain to lead to a lengthy analysis, usually starting with the wind, its speed, its direction, what it might bring with it, the height of the waves, the color of the sky. Then come the "I remember when" stories and the "Can you top this?" anecdotes. To an outsider, the talk of wind and weather seems almost an obsession.

"Had a blizzard down here once," Joe says. He fills a Styrofoam cup with coffee, lays a honey bun in the microwave. "Wind from the north, whitecaps, ton of snow." He slurps his coffee and coughs. "Needs sugar," he says.

It is comfortable leaning against the counter. The store is warm and scented with cinnamon. I am enjoying the companionship of the year-round locals. "When was that blizzard?" I ask.

"It was in . . . You remember what year that was?" Joe asks the cashier.

"No, Joe, I might not have been living down here yet."

Joe is thinking, running through each year's storms in his mind. "Wasn't '94," he says. "That was the hurricane. Could have been '92. Naw, it wasn't '92."

Joe has already finished his honey bun. He licks icing from his fingers as I find myself drifting back into a decade-old memory still vivid with wind and water, my own story about Duck and weather.

Lightning danced around us, and we were thirsty. Four wet hours had gotten us only sixty miles from our home in the Tidewater area of Virginia. We still had twenty left to go. It was a late-August weekend, the traffic inching along the southbound lanes on N.C. 158. We had hit hail in Moyock, the rain so hard in Coinjock it hurt just to think about it. My husband cursed under his breath, checked his watch, tapped the steering wheel. Our son, eight and full of more audible complaints, kicked the back of my seat. The car radio played static between weather reports. The forecast wasn't good.

At ten miles an hour, we made slow progress toward the Wright Memorial Bridge, the gateway to the Outer Banks. Horns competed with thunder. Flashing blue lights brought us to a standstill. A county sheriff directed us around the accident, two cars with dented fenders and broken lights, a hubcap swirling in a puddle.

"A mistake," I said.

My husband nodded. Our son kicked a little harder.

Two lanes narrowed into one. The bridge was just ahead.

"Let's see how long it takes to get over this thing," my husband said. "If we don't get blown off."

A half-dozen car lengths from the bridge, everything seemed to stop. Wipers rubbed the windshield dry. The wind vanished. The kicking halted. I thought our son had fallen asleep.

"Look," he said.

In the distance, a single band of color broke through

the flat sky. It started in the east, one pink ribbon curving over the bridge and dropping into the Currituck. A second followed, yellow as a sunflower. Purple, then blue—the colors formed an archway, a spectrum to welcome us. We drove under a rainbow, thinking it a good omen. It was our first trip to Duck.

By late afternoon, we found the village, six miles north on N.C. 12. Our rental house, a modest A-frame, sat high on stilts atop a sand hill almost midway between the Atlantic and the Currituck. Another storm blew in. A waterfall dripped from the wraparound deck that hugged the second story. There were pools flooding the walkway and puddles ankle deep in the carport. We slept with a northeast wind slamming into the back door and a crooked rain glazing the windows.

We walked barefoot and groggy, the three of us, on Duck's beach by sunrise. We let ghost crabs scuttle around our toes, followed the twisting paths of pelicans diving for their breakfast, examined what was left of a loggerhead turtle that had washed up headless on the shore.

There were predators and prey and a voice in the wind, a reminder that even what wasn't pretty was nature's right and that, like creation itself, all of it was the way it was intended. The world was wet and raw. The wind was sovereign, a mystical force pushing back time. For an instant, everything was just beginning. Sea, sky, land, and animals, all of us were newly born, emerging from a common source. The wind blew us into life, and we took breath, I thought, for the first time.

The cashier is teasing Joe. "Maybe you should buy a shovel."

"Already got one," he says, refilling the Styrofoam cup. "Seen just about everything down here. Can't tell what you'll get in Duck."

Joe taps his rolled papers on the counter. "Better get back home," he says. "Want to see what the Weather Channel is saying. You girls keep out of this wind."

For a half-century after Raleigh's first expeditions, the British kept out of the Outer Banks wind. The frequency of brute storms and heavy ocean overwash and the threat of inlets opening or shoaling made the Banks barely accessible. After England's explorers abandoned their attempts to settle here, they turned their sights north and west. By 1607, colonists found dry land, establishing America's first permanent settlement in Jamestown, Virginia, a more hospitable location. But by the middle of the seventeenth century, a few hundred Tidewater Virginians were venturing south over the line, as if to rediscover these barrier islands. Most of those who decided to stay on the North Banks were rumored to be runaways or pirates. For fleeing outlaws and freedom-seeking indentured servants, the area must have seemed the consummate hideout. A colonial recluse or inland pariah might have mistaken this barren coast for utopia.

Though some of the first Bankers probably earned their notorious reputations, greater numbers of them were legitimate property owners with sizable holdings. The first recorded land grant, issued in 1663, went to Sir John Colleton for the island now known as Colington, which is surrounded by the Currituck, Albemarle, and Roanoke Sounds and situated between Kitty Hawk and the mainland. Other grants followed, generally for large tracts to men of privilege. The majority of the wealthy grantees were investors only. Comfortable gentlemen, they didn't intend to engage in a year-round battle with a riling wind and the unpredictable conditions it created.

Absentee owners with North Banks interests found agents or caretakers to improve or monitor their lands. Colleton seems to have started a tradition that continues on the Banks today: property management. He engaged the services of Captain John Whittie, commissioning him to build a plantation on Colington Island. Trees were felled; houses went up; corn grew; men practiced animal husbandry; hogs and sheep fed on the weeds and wild grass. Later, another of Colleton's agents, Peter Carteret, attempted to grow tobacco, already a local money crop because of its popularity with the

British, whether in England or the colonies. Carteret tried cultivating grapes and drew up plans for a vineyard, but little success or profit came from his ventures.

With the purchase of Outer Banks land came the livestock that inhabited it. Hogs, cows, and sheep provided a stable source of food and employment. Many of the North Banks' first residents made their way as stockmen. Others relocated from New England, like the whalers who competed with the locals for the profits of selling whale oil.

Neither wealthy investors nor runaway servants, some of the first Bankers were poor squatters or men of humble means who claimed a small tract of North Banks sand and tried to build a future on it. They looked for a hill in the woods, trees to shield them from the ubiquitous wind, a high spot to protect them from the Atlantic's surges. They cleared just enough space to build their lumpy log houses, found solace between stands of black oak and groves of tall pine bordering the Currituck. With their wives and children, they dug shallow gardens, fished for blues in the ocean, set crab pots in the sound. In the lean years, they learned that survival meant being stockmen, wreckers, whalers, farmers, and fishermen, all at the same time.

Just how many of these settlers lived in the area that is now Duck is uncertain. Before 1750, recordkeeping made it virtually impossible to know exactly where the first Bankers set down roots. Neither Corolla, Duck, Southern Shores, Kitty Hawk, Kill Devil Hills, Nags Head, nor Hatteras Island had yet been named. At that time, these neighboring communities were known simply as the North Banks. By 1670, they constituted part of Currituck County. Duck, in all likelihood, began with a share of those runaways, squatters, and small landholders, each of them, I like to think, as wayward and determined as the wind and water. They eked out a modest existence, accepting the challenge of this barren beach, subsisting whatever way they could in the space between a reckless sea and a shallow sound, committing themselves to making a community on a narrow strip of sand.

Predictions are that the worst of today's storm won't move in until afternoon. This morning, I woke before dawn to a weather report. Blower was the first word I heard. On the oceanfront, I waited for the late-winter sun to rise and warm the village. Daybreak came, the morning dizzy with wind. The sky was slate, the sea the color of oysters. Breakers trounced the shore, frothing, spitting, lapping at the frontal dunes. Sand raked my hair, grazed my face like crab claws. I lasted long enough to watch two sea gulls fight the wind, then each other, over a broken shell and the piece of meat left inside it, too tiny for me to see or for them to share.

A hostile climate can make men greedy. With resources scarce and livings meager, the first Bankers scoured the beach on days like this, hoping that the wind-fed breakers had pushed a natural or man-made treasure onto the shore. On the North Banks, beach-combers quickly turned into wreckers. A good wrecker worked fast and kept quiet, laying claim to whatever discovery the sea offered him.

By 1678, wrecking had become popular and lucrative enough that Bankers were required to report their findings and share a percentage of their profits with the Lords Proprietors. Legally, wreckers needed a permit to take possession of a beached whale. But on the North Banks, laws broke as regularly as waves. A dead whale brought families with buckets and barrels. Men with no papers hacked off thick slabs of flesh, scraped the carcass clean, yanked muscle from bone. The process could take a week; speed was more important than skill. Then the boiling began, the air rank with the stench of rotting yellow blubber. Women and children lowered one hunk after another into vats and watched them smelt into precious oil.

The Bankers could carve up a foundering vessel more quickly than they could a whale. In a day's time, they stripped off boards, pulled out nails, loaded cargo into carts drawn by horses or dragged by families over the sand hills. They rescued mariners left on board. Often, the beached sailors, like the casings and guts of their ships,

By 1678, WRECKING HAD BECOME POPULAR AND LUCRATIVE ENOUGH
THAT BANKERS WERE REQUIRED TO REPORT THEIR FINDINGS AND SHARE A
PERCENTAGE OF THEIR PROFITS WITH THE LORDS PROPRIETORS. THIS
PHOTO SHOWS THE WRECKAGE OF THE *HELEN BENEDICT* NEAR NAGS HEAD
IN 1914.
Courtesy of the Outer Banks History Center

went back home with the Bankers. The injured could rely on good care. Many wave-beaten bodies restored their health in the back rooms of houses turned into make-shift hospitals. A few of the shipwrecked may have fallen in love with the sweet-tempered daughters who fed them soup or sang them into sleep. Maybe the adventure of this landscape held them, or a lack of funds kept them from returning to their home ports. For whatever reasons, some of those stranded sailors never left the North Banks. A few more houses appeared in the woods; a few more wreckers combed the beachfront after a storm.

Wrecking was profitable but unreliable—a good return for hard work, but only when you could get it. Livestock still provided the main means of survival on the North Banks, a natural range whose ocean and sound were every bit as effective a barrier as the costly fencing needed inland. Those first settlers coveted each grazing head. With little else to depend on, the Bankers relied on the bounty of cows, sheep, and pigs to keep them alive.

In the early 1700s, the Poteskeets encountered white men for a second time. These pale-faced strangers didn't venture to the mainland but stood along the edge of the Currituck Sound watching for the tribal hunters, who, like their fathers and grandfathers before them, came to the North Banks in search of good meat—the same meat the Bankers contended was rightfully theirs. Initially, the Poteskeets may have misinterpreted the shouts of those who waited for their canoes. Perhaps what they heard were merely loud greetings of welcome. It wasn't until they were on the shore of the Currituck that the natives felt the heat of the Bankers' ire. There, they could see how the white men's faces burned red as a summer sunset. The Bankers spoke bitter words and made threatening gestures. The Poteskeets understood the white men's warning: should they ever come back to hunt the North Banks, the only thing they'd find was danger.

The Poteskeets boarded their canoes, crossed the Currituck without incident. Back on the mainland, facing their families empty-handed, they determined they would neither attack nor surrender. Peaceably, the tribe took its troubles to the North Carolina Council, presenting its complaint in writing: "The Inhabitants of Corratuck Banks have and doe hinder ye Said Indyans from hunting there and threaten them to breake their guns, and that they Cannot subsist without the liberty of hunting on those their usuall grounds."

Whether genuinely moved by the tribe's hardships or motivated by the fear of Indian uprisings, the council considered the petition carefully. On March 10, 1715, the issue was ordered: the Poteskeets "henceforward [had] Liberty to hunt on any of the said Banks land." But within a few decades, despite the council's decree, the number of natives dwindled, the next generations blighted by disease, poverty, and displacement. This time, the Poteskeets discovered, the wind had brought more trouble, hostile strangers it forgot to blow back across the sea.

♦♦♦

Outside Wee Winks, the sky hangs heavy, a sack ready to rupture. From the car radio, weathermen chant warnings like mantras: "Gale force winds," "Heavy surf," "Ocean overwash." They forecast a mix of ice and snow and just about guarantee flooding at high tide. I remember Duck's first villagers, how they forfeited homes with oceanfront views in exchange for a blanket of woods and the security of the sound. I understand that old urge, feel drawn to the same shallow Currituck, which, with its shoaling inlets, has protected the North Banks even in wartime.

During the Revolution, British fleets easily penetrated the deep harbors of New England and Hampton Roads, Virginia, but they found the North Banks more challenging. Wind, water, and sand bars thwarted their strikes, threatening to grind their grand ships to a halt. In 1776, as a precaution, colonists living along the Currituck formed small armies. Their principal plan of defense required patrolling thirty-five miles of the sound's shoreline. News that English raiding parties had already begun hijacking merchant vessels and stealing livestock farther south near Ocracoke galvanized bands of untrained soldiers. By 1778, the British worked their way to the North Banks, crossing the Currituck from the mainland. The Currituck militia reclaimed stolen schooners, captured at least two enemy ships, the *Tartar* and the *Surprise*, and took numerous crew members prisoner.

When America's first war finally ended, residents began to recognize the North Banks' real-estate potential. The original owners readily split their few large tracts into smaller parcels for willing buyers, the Currituck courthouse recording sixty-two deeds and grants on the North Banks between 1783 and 1789. But it was wind and water that marked the last years of the eighteenth century. Storm after storm bore down on the coast, residents and visitors recording gale-force winds and tides at least nine feet above the high-water mark. Each squall delivered another beaten vessel, stranding crews and valuable cargoes. The North Banks had become a wreckers' paradise.

By 1801, so many ships had grounded along the coast that the state mandated wreck districts, an early division of neighboring communities along the Outer Banks. The state assigned a vendue master to supervise each district. As commissioners, these masters had numerous responsibilities: taking possession of disabled boats, itemizing and advertising their cargoes, auctioning their contents, and eventually recruiting helpers within the district to assist in the rescue of distressed vessels. But North Bankers weren't necessarily bidding

on auctioned cargoes. The "finders-keepers" ethic of
bygone years remained the favored code of conduct.
Beachcombers, like their daddies before them, knew
how to keep a secret. Anyone discovering a wreck could
haul home the goods days before the vendue master
arrived to take inventory.

The nineteenth century brought another war, more
storms, more shipwrecks. With these years came the
changes—new faces, opportunities, and recognition—
that individualized communities on the North Banks.
By 1850, more than one-sixth of the 3,400 residents
who made the Outer Banks their home lived between
New Currituck Inlet and Jockey's Ridge. Of the 102

North Banks families listed on the census that year, Kitty Hawk claimed at least 40. Duck probably had fewer than a dozen.

In the 1840s, Nags Head began touting itself as a seasonal utopia. Its initial popularity stemmed from the belief that the salty wind and water provided a natural "vaccine" against the malaria outbreaks that plagued the mainland in warm weather. The first Nags Head hotel, the Ocean Retreat, advertised its grand opening in 1841 with a special invitation to "invalids and persons wishing to escape the Summer and Fall diseases."

During the summer months over the next two decades, steamers from Edenton and Elizabeth City, weighed down with passengers and luggage, left the mainland for the day-long trip to Nags Head. Families crowded the decks, the women shielded from the afternoon sun under a canopy of white gauze parasols. The children were restless; the men, having smoked their cigars and exhausted their conversations, strained to sight a dock in the distance. The Ocean Retreat impressed its guests. Visitors went back to the mainland boasting how the sea air and salt water had healed their bodies and restored their spirits. Journalists from as far away as New York traveled by train and boat to the Outer Banks. Marveling at the "scores of people" who sunned themselves on the landing, they praised Nags Head's "bright white cabins," its "dark masses of foliage," and its "evening sky."

BEGINNING IN THE 1840S, STEAMERS FROM EDENTON AND ELIZABETH CITY, WEIGHED DOWN WITH PASSENGERS AND LUGGAGE, LEFT THE MAINLAND FOR DAY-LONG TRIPS ON THE OUTER BANKS. PICTURED HERE ARE PASSENGERS DISEMBARKING AT NAGS HEAD CIRCA 1900.
Courtesy of the Outer Banks History Center

Sandwiched between Currituck Beach and Kitty Hawk, almost twenty miles north of Nags Head, the area that is now Duck grew slowly. More than another century would pass before anyone thought about developing the village into a summer boom town. In the mid-1800s, the public hardly glanced at a community that didn't even merit a name. The meager number of families who made their homes here lived in anonymity, their joys scarce and simple, their hardships private and more plentiful.

One such family was that of Major and Bethony Burgess. Between 1843 and 1855, the Burgesses buried two daughters and one son on the crest of a soundside hill covered with oak and pine and cedar. Today, dozens of those trees have been stripped away, but the Burgess children's graves remain. Partitioned by a white picket fence, they are set apart from the hundred-thousand-dollar building lots for sale in Founders Ridge, one of Duck's newest developments. What few facts are known about the Burgesses are recorded on the headstones of their babies, though the names and dates are nearly worn away. Mary Luisa, born in July 1842, lived less than eight months. In September 1843, just seven months and seven days after the death of her daughter, Bethony gave birth to a son. The couple named him Thomas Rayner. By March 1844, he, too, was dead. Almost a decade passed before the Burgesses buried another child. This daughter lived a little longer than her brother Thomas and her sister Mary. Nancy Allmead Burgess died on September 7, 1855, two months before her second birthday.

By 1861, the nation was at war with itself. For almost five years, personal hardships, sorrow, and carnage typified life below the Mason-Dixon line, including mainland North Carolina. Yet for the most part, the Civil War on the Outer Banks was short lived, lasting only a year. From the start, the Bankers had mixed loyalties. They proved reluctant Confederates. White flags rose from their rooftops whenever troops in blue or gray came to call.

Because every inlet feeding the Currituck had shoaled by the time the Civil War was under way, the North Banks were protected from Union forces. What action the Outer Banks saw of a war that devastated most of the South was localized around Forts Hatteras, Clark, and Morgan, built on the still-navigable Hatteras and Ocracoke Inlets, almost seventy miles south of Duck.

By 1862, having surrendered their strongholds and waterways to the North, the Bankers focused on everyday trials, preserving what little they owned despite nature's twin despots, wind and water. They fished for their supper, built skiffs, mended nets, rescued stranded sailors, tended small gardens, raised livestock.

In the years immediately following the war, Federal troops occupied Hatteras Island, first to provide protection from possible Confederate influences and assaults, then to plan and build an experimental community for black freedmen.

On the upper half of the North Banks, another transformation was already in the making—the steady metamorphosis of the Currituck. With the sound shut off from the Atlantic for almost forty years and the water no longer saline, features were altered: silt replaced sand; flats thickened into marshes; cattails and black needlerush poked through the reeds and cordgrass. With this new habitat came canvasbacks and redheads, teals and ruddies, Canada geese flying in from the North. Waterfowl flocked to the Currituck, affording this community bragging rights that Hatteras and Nags Head didn't have. Wild birds filled empty stockpots, attracted sportsmen, turned wreckers into lodge keepers and guides and fishermen into hunters. A changed Currituck became the covenant, a pledge for the future, the portent of a place called Duck.

On the Outer Banks, a March northeaster can dupe you, turn a noon sky as dark as dusk. By lunchtime, this blower has worked up a big appetite. It craves more action. Sand gives itself up too easily, and the wind searches for other prey. It chases the mist, freezing it into a hard sleet that pelts the ground and coats the marsh like a shower of shattered glass. Each gust sends a shiver through the floor, a shudder through the clap-

board walls. Every burst celebrates a victory, thrash-
ing the brush, whipping the scrub oaks, flailing the reeds
until they lie prostrate. The windows clatter in their
frames. Even the dauntless Currituck seems rankled and
ready to surrender, its troubled waters rushing away
from the bank in a steady retreat toward the mainland.

When this wind will tire and the waters of the
sound will come rushing back is a mystery to me. But
puzzles breed on the Outer Banks. The residents themselves have been reckoned as enigmas since the Civil
War. "Indifferent," one Confederate officer said of
them. "They constitute a world within themselves."
"Queer folks," another wrote.

The reputation those nineteenth-century Bankers
gained isn't extinct just yet. Flashes of it abide here in
Duck, those bygone qualities recognizable in a handful
of natives who still live in the village. Theirs is a distinctive brand of autonomy, a simple wisdom, a gutsy
charisma, a gentle wariness of outside influences and
mainland manners, a generous sense of adventure, a
resilience in the face of change. Their culture is fla-
vored by this quirky climate, this inconstant land. Their
lifetimes are spent seesawing between the threat of gale-
force winds and high tides and the surety of having survived them.

Over the years, dozens of blowers have jangled the
lives of those who call Duck home. This storm is probably no different from the others. But watching snow

fall over the sand, I can't help thinking this northeaster will rattle the village into nightfall, maybe shaking the old stories free, pushing the past into the present, loosening the spirits of Duck's early settlers and raising them up, like wind and water, from the dead of winter.

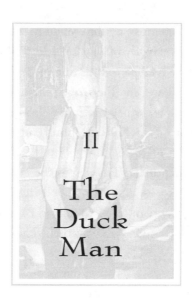

II

The Duck Man

Levin Scarborough knows all about decoys. In Duck, where so many faces have barely ripened into midlife and the majority of the roads, housing developments, and commercial buildings are just breaching adolescence, Levin could almost be mistaken for a decoy himself.

Levin seems suspect, an uncanny replica of the bygone Outer Banks character. Like a human version of the duck hunter's slick, he could be an imposter from the mainland, a modern figure who started out as plain as a block of wood, then was scored and notched into a near-perfect likeness of the genuine Duck old-timer. He could be a parody of the Judas bird of old, a flesh-and-blood lure trained to draw migrating flocks of tourists into the village and the scope of hungry merchants.

Like so many other illusions, Levin appears to be just one more comely development idea in Duck, as carefully rendered as the gables and gazebos and beachfront manors, as coaxing as the coveys of single-story shops that nestle in the woods like ducklings, as charming as each mile of whitewashed clapboard and stretch of plain pine walkway tucked among stands of live oak and red cedar.

For the last two decades, out-of-town investors and high-priced contractors have been carving up the Duck of yesteryear and refashioning it into a contemporary variant of the old-fashioned seaside retreat. What developers haven't knocked down, filled in, paved over, or built up, they have worked to enhance, eventually hiding most of the original Duck under a layer of costly veneer. By 1985, the village of the 1960s and 1970s was barely recognizable, the village of the 1940s and 1950s a mythic ghost.

Today, Duck is built around sun, sand, shopping, and the romance of a lost era. A coat of simplicity has been brushed over every million-dollar deal, a homey quaintness hammered into each joist and floorboard. *Vintage*, planners wanted to prove, could be manufactured, sucked out of one time period and plunked down

LEVIN SCARBOROUGH IS THE REAL THING, A WELL-
WEATHERED NORTH BANKS LOCAL WHO STILL LIKES TO
SIT ON THE FRONT PORCH AND WHITTLE WOOD INTO
WATERFOWL.
Courtesy of Peter J. Mercier, III

into another as easily as sand dug with a backhoe. Selling this new Duck meant capitalizing on what the re-
modeled village offered that neighboring resort towns
along the Outer Banks couldn't. Nags Head neon and
Kitty Hawk commercialism, promoters knew, would
find no place here.

The plan worked. Baby boomers bought up enough of the village to prevail, every one of their alterations heralded in the name of progress. By the early 1980s, Duck was Dare County's latest and greatest boom town. Soon, realtors and shopkeepers were smiling at thousands of new faces every year. And the new faces smiled back. But it was the sheen of a freshly varnished decoy, not the wild, ungarnished Duck, that fetched those tourists and still does, bringing more of them back season after season.

As for Levin, his is another story. He was here before Duck became Duck, before the village churned any fancy thoughts in developers' minds, before this place had a name of its own. An authentic vestige, Levin is the real thing, a well-weathered North Banks local who still likes to sit on the front porch and whittle wood into waterfowl.

❧ ❧ ❧

It's a sun-drenched summer morning, the meridian of the tourist season, the first Saturday of August. Levin, who's been keeping a village vigil for nearly a century, surveys the road. It's early, Levin probably having risen not long after the sun. In another hour, he might be hungry enough to eat breakfast, but it's hard to settle down comfortably at the table when it sounds as if half the world is passing outside your window. Already, the weekend traffic moves like sludge, clogging N.C. 12 in both directions. Levin doesn't need a calendar to know what day it is—another rental week is beginning and ending.

From his workshop garage, Levin can count the cars and vans that stop and start in front of his Duck Road home. If his vision were what it used to be, he might study the faces of the drivers and passengers, inspect the contours of their new Fords and Toyotas, identify the out-of-state license plates, scan the bumper stickers, take mental snapshots of the strangers coming into and out of his hometown.

Levin wears loose-fitting khaki pants with creases sharp as blades, a pressed cotton shirt tucked tight at the waist and opened at the collar, sneakers shining like new. A black ball cap with a stiff visor and the word *DUCK* stenciled across the front shades his face. Levin's usual choice of clothing might qualify as formal summer attire in the village. Here, men typically exchange their forty-hour-a-week desk jobs, their three-piece business suits, and their sturdy wingtips for a few days in the same outfit—a pair of soggy swim trunks, a sweat-stained tank top, a pair of half-laced tennis shoes.

Making a few adjustments, Levin alters his posture, squares into the mannequin pose he will use for watching another day unfold in Duck. In seconds, he can transform himself into a man who might be thirty years younger. The rounded back straightens; the sloped shoulders rise like wings; the neck stretches taut as a swan's. Only his eyes rove, right and left, tracking the southbound exodus and the northbound invasion of minivans and station wagons.

At ninety-four, Levin has sprouts of snowy hair growing over his prominent ears. Glasses perch high on the bridge of a strong nose. His thinning face widens at the jaw. The creases etched into his hollow cheeks could have once been a boy's dimples. But Levin isn't smiling. His mouth is slack, drawn down around the edges like the dramatist's frowning mask. The start of white whiskers shows over his cheeks and chin, the pattern of stubble like a fine coating of sand.

Repeat visitors and the newcomers who live year-round in Duck know Levin's name. They look for him as they pass through the village, sometimes waving at his empty rocker on the front porch or the vacant space next to the workbench in the garage. If it's midafternoon and a wind lulls out of the southwest, Levin may be swaying gently in his wooden, slatted swing. He keeps his back to the road, his eyes on the Currituck Sound, where a few ducks might be gliding just beyond the shallow bank that borders his side yard.

With a mix of reverence and affection, some Duck residents refer to Levin as "Pop." Having lived through just about every occurrence in this North Banks community since its naming in 1909, Levin qualifies as the great-granddaddy of the village. The area's past entwines with his own, one strand seeming inseparable from the other. Levin safeguards volumes of those lost days and decades, stows them away in the archive of memory.

"I can still go back pretty far," he'll say.

A faithful witness, Levin is the living chronicler of this place. He remembers how things used to be. He can tell you how they've changed.

Within the last fifteen years, Levin has become a sort of walking monument, a breathing landmark. Some strangers view him from a distance, waiting for a glimpse of Pop Scarborough in his slow route from house to garage. Some come closer. They spend an hour in idle conversation, eyeing the decoys and seabirds displayed in the front yard. They might even purchase a keepsake from Levin's whittled wooden flocks. At least a dozen mainland journalists and travel writers have dropped in on Levin. Over the years, he has seen his name in print, his every utterance spelled out in black ink, his thoughts arranged into straight columns on white pages.

Levin didn't expect he'd ever become a local celebrity. Reticent but rarely impartial, he chooses words with care. To the litany of questions curious visitors sometimes pose, Levin says what needs to be said but never much more. He shows a tempered congeniality in the midst of his life's interruptions—posing for amateur photographers, letting reporters take his picture while he carves the curve into a mallard's back or dabs paint on the scrawny legs of a heron.

In Duck, Levin seems as much an attraction as the

heads on Mount Rushmore, the geysers at Yellowstone, the battlefields at Yorktown and Valley Forge, though he doesn't seem to understand exactly why. Unsure whether his being a Scarborough from the North Banks, his having lived here almost a century, or his whittling of ornamental decoys has brought about this recent popularity, Levin will tell strangers one thing about which he seems certain: "It's nice to know all of these years I was living in such a fine place."

They call it a "ribbon of sand." They consider it one of the most fascinating land formations on earth. Dozens of geologists, as intrigued with the Outer Banks as some folks are with Levin, have spent years studying this narrow string of low-lying islands off the North Carolina coast. The interest isn't recent, this area having been a source of scientific curiosity for nearly a century. To the theorizing geologist, the Outer Banks are as much mystery as beauty.

Decades of research have precipitated some heated debates. Scientists still argue about how this line of barrier islands came to be, how it got so far from the mainland, how it will or won't survive. On one point, geologists seem to agree: the entire length of the Outer Banks, all 175 miles, is comprised of nothing but sand, layer upon layer of it sculpted and styled by the mighty hands of nature, wind and water.

It is on this Outer Banks sand that Duck's centuries-old genesis came about, its evolution a complex series of temperature shifts and a quirky combination of winds, currents, and storm waves that started almost eighty thousand years ago. During the Ice Age, the sea diminished, its waters drawn away and frozen into glaciers. Within thirty thousand years, the Atlantic sank to a low point, almost four hundred feet below current levels. More land was exposed. The North Carolina coast extended almost twenty miles east of Cape Hatteras, forty miles east of Cape Lookout. One by one, sand ridges ruptured the ocean's shrinking membrane like chicks grown too big for their shells.

Eventually, the world warmed. Glaciers began to loosen twelve thousand years ago, and higher waters gradually returned. The sea kept climbing, and with it, the Outer Banks began to grow, their fledgling bulk nourished by the sand, gravel, and rock flour that great rivers carried across the shrinking coastal plain. At first, the Banks were only spits. In time, they grew into islands, steadily building as the water rose. By 1500 B.C., geologists speculate, the Outer Banks were approximately the size and shape they are today.

〉〉〉

"Family used to own all that land," Levin says, pointing through the line of cars toward Scarborough Lane, spelled *Scarborugh* on the county's new road sign. "Son Gary still lives there."

The Scarborough family goes back almost three

centuries on the Outer Banks. Local legend has it that Levin's distant Scottish ancestors were a hearty seafaring lot who washed up with a crashing breaker on the Hatteras Island beach near Kinnakeet, now Avon, during a summer tempest in the early 1700s. The castaways survived the shipwreck, emerging from the Atlantic as barren as newly exposed sand ridges. They dried beneath the golden sun, weary and empty-handed but not disheartened. If they intended settling on the Banks, they must have wished for more than the shreds of clothing that still clung to them. But all they had were rags stiffened with salt water and the honor they carried ashore with their name. They introduced themselves as *Scarbrough*.

Over the years, their lilting accents waned. They mimicked the ways of other early Bankers, adapting to lives of fishing and crabbing, scavenging the beach after every storm as naturally as the gulls and ghost crabs. In time, they saw their meager assets grow. Even their name spawned another syllable. Soon, the *Scarbroughs* became *Scarboroughs*, and the few begot many.

Scarborough daughters married the sons of Outer Banks families from Kinnakeet, Hatteras, and Kitty Hawk. They bore children with their husbands' names— Meekins, Miller, or Price; Etheridge, Tolar, or Twiford; Austin, Perry, or Whidbee. Scarborough men took wives and seeded new generations, the clan's numbers continuing to mount until there were second, third, and

fourth cousins, a sturdy branch of Scarborough growing in dozens of family trees.

Some of those early Scarboroughs moved inland.
Some may have ventured as far north as Maryland. But
most of Levin's people never left the Outer Banks, his
immediate ancestors migrating less than fifty miles north
of their starting point on Hatteras Island. They set down
their belongings next to the Currituck Sound, laying
claim to some North Banks land not far from the community that eventually became Duck.

Levin's great-grandfather George Scarborough, Sr.,
was born in 1810. He married in 1835 and was the
father of three boys and two girls by 1850. In that year,
the middle-aged George spent most days working as a
seaman, maybe having built his own sloop or saved
enough money to buy one. In partnership with other
seamen from the North Banks, George could have transported light cargoes of fish or wood to the mainland,
navigating a double-masted schooner across the shallow Currituck. Like most Bankers, he probably supple-
mented his income by fishing and wrecking, taking his
eldest sons—Wallis, fifteen, and George, thirteen—to
help pull in nets, drop crab pots, and haul home whatever they caught in the sound or found lying along the
beach. At home, Lovie, George's wife, must have depended on twelve-year-old Mary to help with the cleaning and cooking, the care of her four-year-old brother,
Hilary, and the new baby, Amanda. Almost five years

passed before Lovie was pregnant again. At forty, she gave George a fourth son, Andrew.

In the spring of 1870, George and Lovie still had three of their six children living with them. Sons Wallis and Hilary were already adults, both bachelors who saw little purpose in venturing far from the family nest. The youngest, Andrew, fifteen, was probably growing as fast as panic grass.

Sixty by then, George, Sr., had already given up the work of a seaman. Old-timers on the North Banks knew that nothing was permanent; there were no long-term careers on which they could rely, only work, doing whatever needed to be done day by day to survive. Easy times were a luxury the Scarboroughs rarely knew. With no thought of retirement or the security of a pension, they had only the water. Most seasoned Bankers turned to it, even if it meant resorting to unprofitable trades. An aging George spent his last years fishing, catching at least enough to fill five plates on his family's supper table.

Like sisters Mary and Amanda, the younger George left home. He had given up depending on his parents or the water to support him. Married with two small boys and a baby girl of his own to feed, Levin's grandfather turned to the gritty North Banks land. For a time, he tried cultivating himself into a farmer and his sandy lot into a farm, growing vegetables and raising a few chickens and pigs in a yard probably no more than a stone's throw from the homestead he had known in childhood.

Over the next decade, George must have felt his desire for farming wither like a bad crop. It may have been a constant July sun that blistered the beans or a spring northeaster that drove a killing chill down into the roots of every new seedling. Perhaps it was an early-summer squall that tore the yellow blooms off the squash or ripped the ripening green pods from their lanky vines. It might have been too much salt air that burned the rows of new corn brown or his ailing father's advice that swayed him. Maybe it was his fishermen brothers' persistent reminders that finally convinced him: "We're Scarboroughs. We were born to be on the water."

George let the land lie fallow. Following the path his ancestors had taken, he adopted the work of his father and brothers, eased back smoothly into the ways of the water. Some things, George may have believed, were constant, even on the Outer Banks. A Scarborough, like the legend that came with the name, was inextricably yoked to the sea.

❧❧❧

A hand-painted sign on Levin's garage reads "Pop's Duck Shop." If he has the raw materials, Levin will spend most of the morning carving, probably something with wings. Depending on his mood and his supply of lumber, it could be a Canada goose or a North

A HAND-PAINTED SIGN ON LEVIN SCARBOROUGH'S GARAGE READS
"POP'S DUCK SHOP."
Courtesy of Peter J. Mercier, III

Banks sanderling. By afternoon, he will have fashioned the form of some Currituck bird out of a hunk
of hardwood.

"Like using gum oak or tupelo," Levin says. "But
tupelo is getting mighty expensive these days."

Levin took up whittling a quarter-century ago—
"when I was still young," he says. A distraction, something to pass the time, carving kept Levin's hands busy
after a heart attack forced the rest of him to slow down.
He was sixty-nine. Within a year, he had produced a
handsome collection of hand-crafted waterfowl, mas-
tering just about every species of duck. He also experi-

mented with other creatures, mostly birds, that frequented the North Banks. He carved decoys, ornamental sandpipers and herons, wall plaques in the shape of gulls and geese. He even whittled a few flat fish.

By the early 1980s, Levin's whittling gained momentum. If he wasn't fishing down at the Kitty Hawk pier, he was probably carving. What had started as a therapeutic hobby was looking more and more like a burgeoning business. The garage—one half a whittler's workshop, the other an informal showroom—was getting crowded.

Back then, Levin's workbench was almost always smeared with sticky paint, the floor coated with sawdust and wood chips. Levin might be standing ankle deep in shavings, brushing a second coat of teal green over the flawlessly carved head of a mallard. And right beside him would be Missy, his longtime companion, the good-natured black Lab poking her snout into every detail, sniffing a short trail to each new creation as though it were real prey and she a great huntress.

As Levin worked, trucks lumbered up and down Duck Road, each belching colossus delivering a shudder as it passed the house. Rows of ducks bobbed on the shelves. The windows clattered. Across the street, heavy machinery fractured the landscape. Men in hard hats shouted instructions over the gnawing of chain saws and the crack of splitting timber. Trees fell. Backhoes snarled across newly stripped sand hills. Hammers played percussion to the steady buzz of power drills.

Along with the construction crews that reassembled Duck came an influx of strangers. They looked for building lots, vacation homes on the beach or retirement homes on the sound, all sorts of investment properties. Most ended up buying a piece of Duck, and many seemed to want something they could take home as a reminder of their purchase. It didn't take long before the strangers spied Pop's garage. Levin had customers.

He found the ways of a salesman simple. All he needed to do was whittle and wait. Being an entrepreneur didn't change him. He kept it casual, maybe dozing in his rocker and letting Missy, herself droopy-lidded, mind the shop while wives browsed through the merchandise and husbands leaned against the porch railing. Their big, bare homes in need of decorating, women shoppers usually wanted more than a mallard for the great-room mantel. Pop stocked plenty of herons for the bedrooms and geese for the kitchens, a fish for every bath.

"I guess," Levin once told a reporter about his new venture, "people like to say they got a duck in Duck. That's okay with me."

Levin was right. Most people did buy a duck in Duck, many of those purchases coming right out of Pop's garage. When sales were slow, Levin never resorted to anything fancy—no flashy advertising or Fourth of July specials. Having developed a homespun marketing strategy, he devised a common-sense formula that took the worry out of profit margins and inventory control: "Whatever I make, I buy my wood and supplies with. And do some more whittlin'. If I sell a lot, I buy a lot of supplies. If I don't, I don't."

Levin knew how to keep his overhead in check while his changing neighborhood kept the customers coming. For a while, it must have seemed a perfect union: Levin's canine assistant, his comfortable rocker, that painted sign on the garage, a wealth of newcomers. Week after week, he whittled more and more gum oak and tupelo as developers carved up another mile of beachfront and construction crews cut through a few more acres of Duck woods.

A century before, there were no house hunters, no summer tourists flowing through the village like a human current. The North Banks neighborhood Levin's grandparents knew was scarcely populated at all. Just about everyone who lived there was kin to either a Harris, a Rogers, or a Scarborough. Most working-age men listed on the 1880 census reported their occupation as sailor. George Scarborough, having already abandoned farming, was one of them.

By then, almost two decades had passed since the Outer Banks escaped the wrath of America's most acrimonious war, in which the Scarboroughs' home state was pitted against a government even many mainland Carolinians were reluctant to forsake. With other Bankers, George and his wife, Elebinus, had probably shared a halfhearted interest in Confederate goals. But when the Outer Banks fell to Union forces, they didn't worry. Their years together were marked by more compelling personal concerns: George and Elebinus had three children to feed and clothe, dozens of northeasters to weather, a boat to patch, nets that needed mending, a widowed mother to console and care for, debts to pay, George's grief in the months following his father's death. But each passing season seemed to bring with it some measure of good fortune. Possibilities drifted over the dunes like the call of laughing gulls. The same Civil War that had seared and scarred the Carolina mainland was seeding promises along the Outer Banks.

As early as 1867, the federal government scattered its influence up and down these barrier islands, as if rewarding the Bankers for their unflinching Union loyalties. Better times arrived every month. Paychecks came by boat from Washington. Grants and vouchers gave fishermen enough starting capital to become merchants. On the beachfront, local men worked with saws and hammers instead of nets. Lifesaving stations sprang up like sand spurs. Lighthouses spiraled.

Nature, too, unfolded a generous spirit, particularly on the North Banks, where great bounty lay just beyond the Currituck marsh. Behind stalks of cordgrass and black blades of needlerush were hundreds of ducks. Ruddies, teals, canvasbacks, mallards, and buffleheads skimmed the water or nested on muddy flats. Canada geese descended from the winter skies.

After decades of struggle, the Scarboroughs may have been surprised by their community's budding providence. Good-tasting birds were flocking to their sound, and reliable work was moored on their ocean-front. Serendipity hid behind every barren slope; hope bubbled like sea spray. Yet living on a strip of sand made the Bankers cautious and guarded. They knew that each day depended on the whims of nature—the direction of the wind and the will of the water. Maybe a gentle southwesterly breeze would warm the Banks, leaving behind nothing but blessings for the next generation. Maybe a surging tide would wash every blessing away.

Like all North Banks parents, George and Elcbinus must have been encouraged. They watched for signs, good or ominous, in the sky and the surf, the whole time wishing their children and their children's children benevolent days, long years, a rich future.

❦ ❦ ❦

Before scientists arrived here, nineteenth-century Bankers already understood that the sand spits they lived on were constantly shifting and changing. What latter-day geologists have proven is that this ribbon of sand continually travels toward the mainland. They refer to it as "landward retreat" or "shoreface recession," explaining that most of the movement results from the ever-rising sea.

Industrialization, increased population, and the human tendency to use without putting back have created a greenhouse effect. The earth is heating up again, and the polar icecaps are still melting. Over the last two hundred years, the ocean has risen fourteen inches, most of that occurring since 1890. Geologists estimate that global warming is causing the sea to rise at a rate of three inches per decade, and they expect that rate to accelerate.

With these rapidly climbing waters comes the westward migration of the barrier islands. Duck—like all of the Outer Banks north of Cape Hatteras—is advancing five feet closer to the mainland every year. As the beachfront constantly recedes and erodes, geologists issue their warning: what now rests on top of the sand will eventually lie beneath the Atlantic.

❧ ❧ ❧

By the time Levin's father, Daniel, was old enough to look for work, the United States Life Saving Service had expanded its Virginia-based District #6 to include eighteen new rescue sites along the Outer Banks. One of the original seven stations built in 1873 or 1874 was just a mile or two up the beach from what is now Duck. The Caffey's Inlet Rescue Station, a simple, two-story box of a building, was probably covered in pale cedar shakes or whitewashed pine, topped with a pitched roof, and fringed with a broad porch.

The Caffey's station opened on December 7, 1874. W. G. Partridge was the station's first keeper, a job that paid him two hundred dollars a year. His inaugural crew, a half-dozen Outer Banks locals, lived and worked at the station from December through March. For their efforts, these surfmen earned forty dollars per month during the winter and three dollars for each emergency call they received any other time of year.

Early keepers and crew members were sometimes unprepared or ill-suited for their work. Rescues required men who possessed physical strength and emotional restraint, backbone and muscle, pluck and grit to match the willfulness of a combative sea, wave for wave. The only surfman worth the title was one with the skill and daring to guide a boat through crashing breakers and blinding rainfall. Not every man could endure the strain of knowing that he and his fellow rescuers were always one whitecap away from capsizing.

Long, lonely foot patrols took a surfman across barren miles of wind-beaten beach, a lantern held tight and low and steady after twilight, eyes scanning a vast, black ocean hour after hour, vision dashed by cold and salt and blowing sand. A carpenter, farmer, or stockman might wither away under the stress of the work. This job was best suited for men already used to working on the water—men like the Scarboroughs.

Even when the keepers and surfmen were qualified, rescue attempts in those early years often proved

The Caffey Inlet Rescue Station opened on December 7, 1874.
Courtesy of U. S. Coast Guard

futile. The stations were too far apart, the staffs too small, the months of operation too few.

On November 24, 1877, not far off Nags Head, more than a hundred crewmen clung to what was left of the USS *Huron*. Their wait for rescuers must have seemed interminable, their odds for survival diminishing with each passing second. The local station was desolate; there would be no regular patrol until December. News of the wreck would depend on a few early-morning fishermen. By the time the keeper and surfmen knew of the disaster and boarded the rescue boat, ninety-eight men had drowned. Another five would die after the lifesavers brought them to shore.

Two months later, a battered wooden steamer foundered off the Currituck Banks almost midway between the Jones's Hill and Caffey's Inlet stations. Again, it took hours before lifesaving personnel were aware of the wreck. Like the *Huron* before it, the *Metropolis* lost too many of its crew, eighty-five men swallowed by the Atlantic.

By 1883, the government ordered more stations built, additional keepers and surfmen hired, an increase in the months of operation. At Caffey's Inlet, the changes saved lives and proved the valor of keeper and crewmen. That same year, rescuers at the Caffey's station responded to the wreck of an Italian ship, the *Angela*. Not a single crew member was lost.

Getting a job with the Life Saving Service could

bring a North Banks man benefits beyond pay. With these positions came a certain rank and prestige most Bankers had never experienced. Even uneducated surfmen could become community heroes or popular spokesmen. Neighbors turned to them for answers and guidance. The prestige of a keeper could seem as mighty as the ocean he was hired to watch.

At twenty-four, Daniel Scarborough must have felt the challenge of the Atlantic, each cresting wave a dare by the neighborhood bully. He probably grew up idealizing the rescuers' rugged lives and spent some part of each boyhood day wandering over the dunes with his brother George. Imagining a future spread as wide as the beach, Daniel may have felt his blood rush with the thought of shipwrecks, sensed a surging confidence that his deft handling could steer a surfboat over a roiling sea. Heart racing and palms clammy, he'd envision himself reaching out and clasping the hand of a drowning man. He'd smile thinking about the august legacy that would follow him back to shore. Honor drove the desire to be an Outer Banks surfman. But even the practical boy in him might have been lured by the reliability of government pay vouchers that accompanied such work

Soon, another voice beckoned Daniel. This one came from across the Currituck. The girl he loved was raised on the mainland. Daniel called her Etta, not Mary, the name her parents had given her. In 1887, Etta left her home in Coinjock, marrying Daniel and adapting to her new life on the North Banks.

By the turn of the twentieth century, brothers Daniel and George Scarborough were both working men with families to support. Each had three children, the cousins close enough in age to be constant play-mates. George found his livelihood as a waterfowl hunter on the Currituck, but Levin's father headed back to the sea. Choosing lifesaving as his profession, Daniel had a career that spanned a quarter-century as a surfman at the Poyners Hill and Corolla stations.

❧ ❧ ❧

Daniel and Etta's fourth child, Levin Scarborough, was born on the first day of spring in 1904. Since then, he has spent all but thirteen years of his life in Duck. In 1941, he moved his family to Virginia, but it was necessity and not choice that took him away. A carpen-ter and cabinetmaker, Levin met up with some close-fisted years and meager earnings. Forced to look for work on the mainland, he found a job at the Norfolk Naval Shipyard. After his youngest daughter, Betty, graduated from Kempsville High School, he came home. Levin hasn't considered leaving the village since.

"Built this house when we got back in '54," Levin says. "Course, none of this was here then." Levin uses his head like a pointer, first motioning across the way to the shops at Scarborough Faire, then next door to the Swan Cove, a recently built eatery bordering the

Currituck, a rambling white structure set back from the road and glistening like a shell.

"Used to be, you knew your neighbors. Now, you never see the faces of the people who build right next to you. I don't much like the growth, but I'm too old to run. I'm just going to have to stick it out."

There was a time when Levin recognized every face in the village, many of the residents related to him by blood or marriage. Back then, knowing was easy. "In 1915," he says, "there were only twelve families living around here." Levin can reach back a little farther, into memories of his early childhood, when this area was known only as a "neighborhood" on the North Banks. But for most of his life, Levin has identified the place he calls home as Duck.

Some folks say Duck officially began with a tin box. Almost ten years into a new century, the miles between Caffey's Inlet and Martin's Point remained untitled. It was Lloyd Toler who decided to submit a petition to Washington. He wanted a neighborhood post office, and if he could get permission to open one, his neighborhood would finally have a name all its own. Already reading the paperwork and studying the guidelines, he printed the application in his best hand, carefully filling in each block until he got to the lines that required the petitioner to list three possible names for his community.

Toler thought about it for a time. Problem was, he

could come up with only a single suggestion. In his mind, there was only one name suitable for this place, and it certainly fit the government recommendations— "Choose a name," the guidelines said, "neither too long nor too hard to spell." Just about anyone who saw the ruddies, teals, and canvasbacks would have chosen the same name Toler finally put on that petition: he printed the word *Duck*.

Waiting for a decision to come from the capital was the only step left. When it finally arrived on June 29, 1909, Toler stepped off the landing with a metal box. He kept it locked, held it tight and close to his chest, walked slowly, then picked up his pace, almost swaggering by the time he reached the store he owned. It wasn't every day that a man from the North Banks was given a government job and carried the contents of a United States Post Office in his hands.

The next morning, Toler was the area's first postmaster, his store the first post office in the newly named village of Duck.

A little more than a decade later, Duck residents faced another change. Their notification letters came through the mail. In 1920, the North Carolina General Assembly, thinking it easier and more cost effective for all of the North Banks communities lying south of Corolla to be in one county, plucked Duck out of Currituck and gave it to Dare. After that, Daniel Scarborough, like other villagers, had to spend a day in traveling to and from the Dare County Courthouse in Manteo, making the trip at least once a year to pay taxes on the wooded land he owned, the same ground that Levin grew up on, the same lots that are now covered with shops and signs and cars and people.

"Back then," Levin says, "you could've bought up this whole place for three dollars an acre."

Levin has kept track of the soaring prices in Duck; he's seen the land change hands. Now, most of his old neighbors—some friends, some family—have died, and he has watched his old neighborhood fade. But for Pop Scarborough, some things remain constant. There's his wife of seventy years, Ethel, no less beautiful to Levin today than she was at fifteen when he married her in the Methodist church down the road. On a good day, she'll rock with him on the front porch or fill the spot next to him on the slatted swing in the side yard. There's the Currituck Sound, still behind the house, still a good spot for resting in the shade, for counting ducks on the still water, for admiring a blue sky turning tangerine at sunset. There's his family, five of his seven children still living, still coming for supper or an afternoon visit. And there's whittling, shaping something that could almost be real out of a hunk of hardwood.

As for the village, Levin is getting used to the way it fills up and empties out. This morning's parade of slow-moving traffic is not much different from any other summer weekend. By ten o'clock, the sky is a smooth blue crystal, the air hot and heavy. A horn beeps. Sun flashes on chrome. Levin raises one hand to his face, either as a shield against the glare or a meek wave. Then he drops his shoulders, lowers his hand, fixes his focus past the traffic to the street with the misspelled sign.

"Was born right over there," he says.

Without blinking or turning around, Levin steps back slowly, his figure shrinking away from the heat and the noise of the choking road. Inside the garage, a few decoys wait for a coat of varnish. Today, Levin finds no wood chips, no shavings, no splattered paint beneath his feet. Only puddles of cool darkness stain the clean concrete floor as he retreats into the shadows.

III

Outsiders

It is the last week of the winter of 1969, and astronaut Rusty Schweickart is traveling 120 miles above the earth's surface in the *Apollo 9* capsule. A thick cover of clouds makes much of the eastern United States look hazy through the lenses of Schweickart's Hasselblad camera. At ten o'clock, he's still searching for a clear view. Then he sees the North Carolina coast, a strand of sandy spits so fine and faint they might be a stray gray hair on the viewfinder. But Schweickart recognizes the Outer Banks, and he takes the shot.

Later, *Apollo 9*'s images of earth lead the evening news, giving America something to smile about, a sense of national pride in a decade when smiles about being American seem as rare as bobbysocks and poodle skirts and peace of mind. Maybe Duck villagers are watching this modern marvel, an aerial picture of the Outer Banks broadcast all over the country, a snapshot of home taken from somewhere above heaven itself and televised on three major networks.

Photographed from space, the Outer Banks look like child's play, a sketch made with yellow chalk in an unsure hand, the profile of a huge gull, wings spread full for a flight off the edge of a fractured world and into a cushion of sea. One wing reaches above the bird's head; the other stretches below it. Duck is near the tip of the upper wing, where the Currituck narrows and the North Banks bend a little closer to the mainland. On the gull's head, rounded and protruding farther into the Atlantic, the Scarborough family's residence is said to have begun. Thrust forward, the gull's beak tapers to an apex at Cape Point, not far below the Cape Hatteras Lighthouse. Beginning at Ocracoke Inlet and gently curving back toward land, the gull's lower wing is clipped at Cape Lookout. From this vantage point, Duck appears no bigger than a single speck lost in a vast blue background, a place as alien to the villagers as the face of the outsider who took its picture.

But an image of Duck sent from space wasn't the

only thing that didn't ring familiar anymore.

By 1969, the watershed decade of twentieth-century America was finally narrowing to its close. The adrenaline rush had left the nation restless. Americans watched the tightly wound reality they had known in the 1950s unravel week by week. Newspaper headlines made heads turn. Assassinations, racial unrest, and a young generation's dissidence flashed like flares across television screens. Too many sons were leaving their fathers—for the war in Southeast Asia or the sanctuary of the Canadian border—some only physically, others philosophically as well. Too many daughters were denouncing their mothers' rules, rejecting their mothers' lives. Flags still flew in front of public schools and government buildings, but not even those banners of national unity could protect a country charged with political and cultural dynamite. Sparks flew. The Stars and Stripes ignited as easily as old rags.

In 1969, North Carolinians living on the Outer Banks waited like the rest of the country, hoping their state's sons would be the ones coming home alive from the sulky swamps of Vietnam. That same year, local chronicler David Stick was living on Colington Island, doing what he often did, finishing a manuscript, this one for the North Carolina Historical Commission, a book with a simple title, *Dare County: A Brief History*.

As elsewhere, changing times affected much of the Outer Banks. The tourist industry that had begun more than a century before experienced a renaissance after World War II. By the late 1960s, fewer and fewer unexplored areas were left in Dare County. Duck, still a dozen miles and ten years out of the surveyors' field of vision, hid like a ghost crab in daylight. Now, Nags Head and Kitty Hawk were putting the twinkle in developers' eyes. Better bridges, wider highways, new construction, and well-timed publicity drew the curious—buyers and renters with big dreams and open checkbooks. Several members of the Dare County Board of Realtors worried as they watched the growth. Zealous development could add up to big profits and big gains, but a few saw something ugly in the final sum—too little planning plus too much growth could equal a threat to the region's future. David Stick was one Dare County realtor who understood the dangerous math.

Twenty-five years later, in the foreword to the third edition of *Dare County: A Brief History*, the North Carolina Historical Commission credited David Stick as being "the foremost historian of the Outer Banks." But even a newcomer to the region would need no official endorsement to identify the man locals consider their expert. Ask most natives along the Outer Banks about the origins of this or that community, and they will undoubtedly offer the same advice: "You should talk to David Stick."

America's roaring decade was about to come to a

gasping halt. It was 1929, only months before the market crash, and the Sticks were making final arrangements. Relocating to North Carolina meant they had to leave their home in Interlake, New Jersey, where David's father, Frank, had once served as mayor. Settling first in Skyco, a little community on the western side of Roanoke Island, the Stick family may have never suspected that, as outsiders, they would cull so much local and regional attention.

Several years before moving his family, Frank Stick had visited the Outer Banks. What began as a hunting and fishing trip quickly developed into a love affair, Stick's mistress a string of islands as pure as a virgin. Wind-swept beaches, thick marshes, and ample woods—the attraction was a powerful one, and he wanted to own a piece of the place.

Taking a mortgage for a strip of sand may have seemed a risky venture to some, but it was one that Stick and other Northerners, particularly those from the New Jersey Shore, willingly took. He and friend Allen Hueth were buying up Outer Banks land by 1927. Among their initial purchases was the site of the history-making flight of Orville and Wilbur Wright. The investors' first hope must have been that their Southern speculations would eventually take off and prove sturdy enough to bring healthy financial returns. But there was something else that drew outsiders to these sandy shoals. At seven, David Stick felt the allure the first time he saw the Outer Banks: it was an open, clean, happy place.

Before becoming a resident, David understood what visiting the Outer Banks could offer a boy. "For the 25th anniversary of the first flight, December 17, 1928 . . . ," he wrote, "I had the thrill of meeting Orville Wright and of riding in the back of a pick-up truck from Virginia Dare Shores to Kill Devil Hills with Amelia Earhart Putnam, the famous aviatr[ix]."

The Sticks adopted the North Carolina coast as their home. Though they weren't natives of the barrier islands, Frank and David fit as naturally as ospreys and sanderlings. Long before David embarked on the writing career that would eventually bring him statewide celebrity status, the Stick family name was inscribed in the contemporary history of the Outer Banks, Duck included.

David was already developing a sound appreciation for nature, a trait instilled by Frank, a commercial artist who had tired of his career in magazine advertising. Creatively, Frank Stick probably drew new breath on the Outer Banks. The unspoiled environment, the abundance of wildlife, and the development possibilities must have seemed nearly perfect. Finally, he might satisfy his eclectic interests, fulfill his role as a nature artist and conservationist, help sculpt a barren shoreline. This was a place for starting over. Yet not all of the coming years would prove as generous to Frank as his first Outer

Banks visits had been.

Today, Frank Stick is remembered by many as a man of vision and action, a catalyst for growth on the Carolina coast, and the founder of Southern Shores. Wholly committed to the Outer Banks, Frank had big plans and just enough know-how to turn most of them into reality.

During the Depression years, he made his initial move by spurring a government initiative to save the barrier-island beaches. Their survival was threatened by overwash and blowing sand. In 1940, the National Park Service published an official study reporting that "unless certain steps [are] taken toward control of the drifting sands, a vast area [will] be lost." Ten years earlier, Frank Stick had made the same assessment. He began working on a strategy to reverse the results of a naturally hostile environment and ongoing human error. For decades, the Bankers had been depleting the area's protective forests, nearly exhausting the ample supply of wood for use in homes, boats, and even a few logging businesses. As common practice, they allowed their livestock to graze freely along the beaches, the result being that ground vegetation that had once flourished naturally began to vanish faster and faster every year as herds and their appetites grew.

By the turn of the twentieth century, with little having been done in the way of replenishing what forests and vegetation were lost, conditions deteriorated.

Without trees and plants, the Atlantic winds met little resistance. Blowing sand eventually eroded the beaches and clogged the inlets. Travel and fishing proved difficult or dangerous. Every high tide posed a threat of washing over the entire breadth of this thin and vulnerable landmass. The population dwindled; the livelihoods of those who remained waned. Nothing, it seemed, would survive if the traditional practices of the Bankers were not reversed and the forces of nature taken seriously.

By the early 1930s, conditions on the Outer Banks menaced those who called the area home. Like the rest of the nation, North Carolinians living on the coast suffered from the economic hardships of the Great Depression. But Bankers, usually unaffected by mainland troubles, had more to worry about than a lack of jobs. The very land on which they stood was in jeopardy. The surface erosion that had begun to affect the Banks thirty years before was reaching crisis proportions, particularly on the lower Banks. "At Cape Hatteras," David Stick later wrote, "the shore had cut in so severely that the lighthouse was threatened by the sea."

Frank Stick needed the Outer Banks to endure. As an environmentalist, he may have felt compelled to rescue and restore the region. As an investor and developer who envisioned the creation of a national seashore park, he may have seen his hopes dissolving, a potential seaside paradise evolving into a desolate strip of blowing sand and ocean overwash where nothing would be left to attract Northern tourists or guarantee a future for natives.

In 1933, just weeks before the first of two unnamed hurricanes nearly blew Duck off the map, Frank Stick wrote a series of articles detailing his plan to save the Outer Banks. On July 21, 1933, the *Elizabeth City Independent* ran the first of these articles under the headline "A Coastal Park for North Carolina." Initially, Stick's proposal met little opposition. Few Bankers could bristle at a plan that promised to reclaim and secure the lost shoreline, save their property, and provide wages to local men hungry for work in an era of unemployment.

Frank Stick's plan provided the impetus for stabilizing the beaches from Corolla to Ocracoke. In November 1933, the Civil Works Administration committed over a million dollars to help fund the project.

What the Banks first needed were better dunes, ones high, wide, and secure enough to protect in-lying areas from the Atlantic's constant and powerful huffing, puffing, and spitting. Imitating the design of special fences he had seen used to control snow accumulation in the Northeast, Frank Stick built a prototype, a simple construction of brush and scrap lumber.

With the money and the mechanism for building dunes in place, it was time to recruit the labor. Hundreds of men were glad to construct miles of fencing along the shore. In April 1934, the government built a transient camp in Nags Head, where the work would begin. Over the next four years, fifteen hundred men restored nearly 125 miles of Outer Banks coastline. Some dune builders were locals who volunteered to help construct fences, but many more were paid employees, men who could finally earn a few years of wages as a result of Roosevelt's New Deal.

It was during this period that Duck's population surged, the village becoming a temporary home for over a hundred dune builders in the mid-1930s. Tucked into an area known as Duck Woods, not far from Martin's Point, was a government-established workers' compound, long rows of little camps with four men in each, a mess hall, and a canteen. The pay was meager, about five dollars a week. While the government took responsibility for providing the laborers with housing and food, Duck villagers took it upon themselves to provide the hospitality.

During the day, the Duck transient-camp workers, like those in neighboring communities, erected fences introduced by Frank Stick. His design and positioning instructions varied only when wind direction, sand type, or formation patterns dictated. Building dunes on the Outer Banks wasn't as difficult as it was time consuming. The work required patience, precision, and repetition. First, a long row of fencing was fixed into the almost-barren shore. Nature readily complied. The winds blew sand in every direction—from sea to sound,

sound to sea, billions of tiny, trapped grains rising
around the fences, smooth mounds forming in front of
and behind them. Once the sand reached the top of
the fences, workers built another layer of fencing atop
the small, newly formed dunes. More sand blew and
was trapped, which caused the mounds to grow steadily
in height and width. The process of adding new fencing
and trapping multiple layers of blowing sand continued
until the dunes reached a sufficient elevation. Eventually, a high, wide dune rose along the coast, a new wall
of sand separating the sea from residential areas.

At the Duck transient camp, the dune builders relaxed after their full days of work. Many nights, they welcomed a small but enthusiastic community of locals. The visiting men and their government accommodations brought a novel change to the lives of village residents. The compound canteen—a recreation center with lights powered by a generator, as well as a few pool tables—must have seemed a veritable amusement park in a place where electricity was still years away. A bright spot in an otherwise dark period, the canteen fostered camaraderie and fellowship, offered entertainment and an introduction to modern ways of living. Camp workers shared stories, games of billiards, and the ample government-issued supplies—candy bars, soda, ice cream, and beer—with Duck villagers.

Fifty years later, long after the workers had left Duck, Suzanne Tate recorded her mother-in-law's recollections of those times: The transient camp "was a great thing for the people of Duck . . . ," said Ruth Scarborough Tate. "Everyone in the neighborhood enjoyed moving pictures once a week at an outdoor theater at the camp. A whole bunch of us piled in trucks to go to the shows. They were the first moving pictures people at Duck ever saw."

Not all Bankers were as happy with the dune project as the villagers in Duck. Opposition to the new dunes blew in like another hurricane. Some Bankers saw the fences and dunes growing around them as just another attempt to harness their fierce and hard-earned independence. What they said was that they could no longer see the ocean. What they meant amounted to much more. Even before the fences went up, the government had imposed its power; it was the sort of intervention and interference to which many Bankers had long been opposed. With the stroke of a pen, a select group of outsiders put a stop to the open grazing of livestock in 1935. In protest, dissatisfied Bankers tore down fences as soon as they were erected. These acts of vandalism slowed progress, but they couldn't halt it. By 1938, six hundred miles of dune fence lined the North Banks.

David Stick has written about the success of those attempts to build dunes using the fences his father designed: "Where those first low zig-zag sand fences were erected on a flat beach in the vicinity of the Nags Head Coast Guard Station, there is today a line of stabilized dunes, covered with beach grass and sea oats, averaging 150 feet in width and 15 [feet] in height." In its records of the dune-building project, the National Park Service itemized the magnitude of the plan that started with Frank Stick—115 miles of barrier dunes, 141 million square feet of grass, 2.5 million trees and shrubs, 4 million square feet of brush and mulch.

Though Frank Stick helped save the beaches, he couldn't salvage his initial investment in almost twenty miles of Outer Banks property. He had trouble selling lots on the Virginia Dare Trail, in a development he named Croatan Shores, north of Kitty Hawk. David, the recorder of his father's successes, has not forgotten his father's failures. Frank Stick was forced to relinquish most of what he owned in Kill Devil Hills, Salvo, Nags Head, and "other small pieces of property, from Duck to Avon, which in most cases were taken over by former fellow-investors from the Jersey Shore, or were bought at the courthouse door by local businessmen."

⁂

It's a cold but bright afternoon in February, and David Stick has offered to answer a few questions about the subject he knows best—the history of coastal North Carolina. At seventy-seven, Stick still leads an active life, maintaining a home-based office in a second-floor loft. Something or someone always seems to demand Stick's attention. Now, he welcomes a curious visitor into his waterfront house in the village of Kitty Hawk.

Small, unassuming, thin, and balding, Stick has a physical bearing that belies the strength of his influence. It seems he should be bigger, meatier, louder. His voice is soft, sure, and steady, and his eyes, though aided by a pair of thin, wire-rimmed glasses, sparkle like the Currituck Sound pictured in realtors' promotional brochures.

From Stick's living room, Large Colington, a lobster-shaped island accessible by bridge, is visible in the distance. Through a half-wall of glass overlooking Kitty Hawk Bay, Stick points to a wide expanse of patchy grass and sand that serves as his front yard. "The Wright brothers," he says, "once landed right there."

Paintings decorate the walls of the home. Each reveals another dimension of Frank Stick, an artisan who could find his muse in a fisherman and his catch, a hunter and his hound, a bluefish emerging from a foam-tipped wave. Here, there remains little doubt about a father's influence on his son, traits and training flowing from one generation to the next. Like Frank, David has spent a lifetime exposing what most can't see or know without the aid of an artist's curious mind and searching eye. His books, drawn with facts and shaded with local lore and legends, are as illustrative of the Outer Banks as his father's canvases.

Stick likes to talk history. He'll chat at length about other people, but he shows little interest in talking about himself. His autobiography is an abbreviated and candid one.

"I went to the University of North Carolina for one year and flunked out," Stick says without reservation. "I've always been interested in writing, and that's what I was doing there."

Stick's professional writing career started several years before his brief tenure at the University of North Carolina, where, as a freshman, he worked on the college's publications to the exclusion of almost everything else. At fifteen, he was already a reporter, hired by the *Elizabeth City Independent* as its Nags Head correspondent. After his short stay at the university, Stick worked for radio commentator Fulton Lewis, Jr., covering the Washington beat, then served in the United States Marine Corps as a combat correspondent during World War II. Before returning to the Outer Banks in 1947, he was associate editor for *American Legion Magazine*.

In large portion, Stick has devoted his energy to the history of coastal North Carolina as a researcher, writer, or editor of eleven books. He has recorded and lived much of this century's local history. Over the years, Stick, like his father before him, has been an active participant in shaping the Outer Banks—as a real-estate broker, a member of planning commissions, a force in local politics. He continues to maintain an interest in environmental issues and the ongoing development of Dare County. His historical research—a notable collection of correspondence, business records, photographs, Life Saving Service and Coast Guard wreck reports, maps, charts and notes—amounts to more than 150 cubic feet. Added to this are the more than twenty thousand books and pamphlets he has collected over the years. His personal library, the third-largest in North Carolina, includes original documents dating back to the 1800s.

Stick doesn't boast—about his accomplishments or his collection—but he is protective of what he's amassed and preserved. He's happy to have found a new home for his research materials in a place where he knows it will be cared for, appreciated, and shared with those who are susceptible to what his father used to call "a contagious love of the Outer Banks." Ten years ago, Stick offered his research library to the state, but this gesture of generosity had certain conditions about which he was unwavering. "I gave them my library," Stick says, "with the understanding that they would build a facility here to house it and allow it to be used as a research center."

Readily accepted by the North Carolina Department of Cultural Resources, Stick's donation of documents, books, and his father's paintings served as the foundation for the Outer Banks History Center, which occupies a site adjacent to the *Elizabeth II* in Manteo. Open to the public since 1989, the center employs four full-time staff members and a host of student interns. Continuing to build its collection, it adds newly acquired layers to the substantial base Stick provided. In mentioning the center, Stick remains matter-of-fact concerning his connection to its genesis. He focuses attention on the center's former director, Wynne Dough, a scholar and historian whom Stick credits with "a photographic memory" and praises as "exceptional," "brilliant," and "eccentric."

Stick hasn't researched or written much about Duck, but he mentions the village in *The Outer Banks of North Carolina*, published in 1958 by the University of

North Carolina Press. "I don't have much specifically on Duck," he says almost apologetically, "because there wasn't much doing in Duck. This was a very small place as compared to Nags Head and Kitty Hawk. There was a little community with a post office and I think one store. Maybe at one time, there was a second one. It was in Currituck County early on. When Dare was expanded to include Duck, well, by that time, I was visiting Duck, and the only road was on the sound side. It was sand, an old trail that ran along the sound and then back up into the woods. At that time, I would say, there might have been fifty residents."

Stick reels off a few old family names connected with Duck as quickly as a father might those of his children—Beal, Scarborough, Whitson—but he pauses at the name *Tate*.

"Tommy Tate," Stick says, "was a little, stocky, cocky fellow," the kind of man who, bare chested on the coldest day in winter, would stand outside his Duck cottage facing the sound-side road just to prove his mettle. No longer living, Tommy Tate played a role in Outer Banks history, not because he was a tough Banker who could endure a blast of February wind off the Atlantic but because his stories made him popular with two brothers visiting from Ohio.

Tommy's picture can be found in several books about Kitty Hawk's famous aviators and their 1903 flight—which, Stick is quick to remind, "really took

ORVILLE AND WILBUR WRIGHT MADE TOMMY TATE (PICTURED ABOVE)
MEMORABLE BY MENTIONING HIM IN THEIR LETTERS BACK HOME. THEY
CHARACTERIZED HIM AS "A SMALL CHAP THAT CAN TELL MORE BIG YARNS
THAN ANY KID OF HIS SIZE."
Courtesy of the Library of Congress

place in Kill Devil Hills." Scanning the shelves in his living room, Stick looks for—but can't put his hands on—a book with Tommy's photo. He well knows the Tate family name, has written about the Tates and their special connection to the Wright brothers: Captain Bill Tate of Kitty Hawk wrote a letter to Wilbur Wright on August 19, 1900, that initiated the brothers' trip to Dare County; Addie Tate, Bill's wife, known for her good food and hospitality, volunteered her sewing machine to help get the first glider running; Dan Tate, Tommy's dad, assisted the aviators on many occasions. Stick believes that Dan Tate may have originally come from Duck.

At nine or ten, Tommy Tate had already mastered the art of fishing. Balancing a man-sized straw hat on the back of his head, he wore baggy pants rolled up to the knees and held on with a pair of wide suspenders. Justifiably satisfied with his catch on an October day in 1900, Tommy started for home, passing Orville and Wilbur, who had been in Kitty Hawk only a little over a month. He stopped for a visit.

Tommy liked telling stories, especially to these newcomers with big plans about putting a flying machine in the air. It didn't take long before Wilbur and Orville knew Tommy's sports—fishing and storytelling. They admired his skill in both. Orville quizzed Tommy about his knowledge of local gossip.

"Who's the richest man in Kitty Hawk?" Orville asked.

"Dr. Cogswell," Tommy answered with confidence. "How much has he?"

After thinking for a minute, Tommy answered, "Why, his brother owes him fifteen thousand dollars."

Orville and Wilbur made Tommy memorable by mentioning him in their letters back home and by photographing him. They called him "Tom the fisherman" and characterized him as "a small chap that can tell more big yarns than any kid of his size." The Wrights had little trouble convincing Tommy to pose. He seemed hungry for attention. With the brothers' glider behind him, Tommy stood, barefoot and solemn faced. A drum fish half the length of his body hung limply from his hand, its head resting on the ground.

Stick's clearest recollections of Duck are from the early days after World War II, when few people had reason to travel here. He rarely came to Duck until the 1960s, and then only as a route to the beaches beyond the village in Currituck County. "People didn't go much to Duck," Stick says. "They just didn't go. There wasn't much in Duck for them to go to."

Traveling through Duck in the 1940s and 1950s demanded a fair share of courage. The road was rough. Packed sand and nothing more, it required a sturdy vehicle with sound tires and a high chassis. Between 1941 and 1965, there were other dangers as well. "There were bombs," Stick recalls.

What is now the Army Corps of Engineers research

facility overlooking the pier in Duck was once a navy bombing range. Stick remembers those days. "They used Duck for a practice bombing run. They'd drop bombs that would explode enough so that they could see the smoke. But," he adds, "they could kill you. In order to get through Duck after the war, you'd reach the bombing range, and you would have to be very damn careful or you'd have a plane coming in right over your head and dropping these little bombs."

At the mention that falling bombs may have scared visitors away from Duck, Stick's eyes twinkle. He chuckles. "It was exciting," he says. "I ducked them many times."

Hunting bombs in Duck became a regular nocturnal pastime for area boys, some of whom traveled to the village from as far away as Elizabeth City. They'd search the deserted beaches, hoping to find and bring home a military artifact. A few of those boys may have come upon more than World War II-era souvenirs. Rumors still circulate concerning accidents, including one story, popular for almost thirty years, about a young man from the mainland whose hand was partially blown off after the bomb he discovered and brought home detonated. Even now, the shifting sands on Duck's beaches occasionally allow one of the bombs to surface. *Danger* signs remain posted around the periphery of the Duck facility; government plans to remove the bombs have been in effect for the better part of a decade.

"For the third time," Stick says, the sound of disgust thick in his voice, "the military is now coming in and cleaning it all up, again."

In January 1997, the North Carolina edition of the *Norfolk Virginian-Pilot* ran a story about the Army Corps of Engineers and its invitation to village residents to attend a meeting at the Duck Fire Department. The corps wanted to discuss the status of buried bombs still left in Duck. The preceding year, the corps had removed more than three hundred pieces of ordnance, a mixture of unexploded bombs, missiles, and rockets. Yet it acknowledged that there remained the threat of additional hazardous material. Bill Birkemeier, then chief of the Duck facility, felt confident that there were no "high explosives" but emphasized the risky nature of old ordnance that is never certain to stay buried. Fewer than fifty of the bombs the corps retrieved had to be detonated, and those were what Birkemeier described as "less-powerful practice charges."

Another Army Corps of Engineers representative, Judy Wilson, compared the buried bombs to rattlesnakes. "If you don't bother [them]," she said, "[they] won't bother you."

Most of the navy's old practice bombs are half-foot-long missiles with fins and rusty pipes. Every now and then, homeowners use them as lawn decorations. Cleaned and polished, these ornamental metal canisters look to the untrained eye like modern sculptures.

IT WAS DURING THE 1960s WHEN THE NAVY SLOWED DOWN ITS BOMB RUNS ALONG THE DUCK BEACH AND BOYS FROM NEIGHBORING TOWNS STARTED THEIR BOMB COLLECTIONS. THE PHOTOGRAPH ABOVE SHOWS THE OLD DUCK BOMBING AND STRAFING RANGE AROUND 1950.
Courtesy of the Outer Banks History Center

Though the danger of Duck's buried bombs isn't high, the expense connected to their continual emergence is; the Army Corps of Engineers estimates that this newest cleanup will cost more than four hundred thousand dollars.

It was during the middle 1960s when the navy slowed down its bomb runs along the Duck beach and boys from neighboring towns started their bomb collections. By then, David Stick and his family owned a cottage in Southern Shores, a community to which the Stick name is well adhered. Among his other ventures, Frank Stick is credited with creating the town; the story of his 2,600-acre purchase for $30,000 in the late 1940s is a popular one. "For someone who had lost his one-half interest in more than a mile of ocean-to-sound property in south Nags Head because he couldn't pay his $1,500 depression-era loan," David writes, "this was an especially bold move, for the terms of the option dealt with dollar figures previously unknown on the Outer Banks."

Frank Stick gave Southern Shores its name. By 1947, the legal papers were signed and sealed. The same year, David found his way out of New York and back to the Outer Banks. Frank had asked that his son come home to establish a development company, and David agreed to help plan Southern Shores, design its houses, sell its lots. Initially, the arrangement looked promising; David formed Kitty Hawk Enterprises with family friend Bill Coppage. But he didn't stay long. Stick doesn't elaborate on the details of the split, but he alludes to what ultimately drove him to resign his position at Kitty Hawk Enterprises: "The father-son working arrangement did not turn out well, and the following year, I left the company and became an independent real-estate broker."

Without his son's assistance, Frank persisted, paying close attention to the area's zoning. Eventually, he transformed those twenty-six hundred acres into a year-round community. This and the incorporation of Southern Shores in 1979 may account for its current residential population of more than fifteen hundred, a relatively large number by Outer Banks standards.

Today, Southern Shores is Duck's prestigious next-door neighbor to the south, a forerunner of the village's own development. Having researched its history, Stick describes the area as "one of the first to be settled extensively on the North Banks," its deeds dating back to the late 1780s. Now, established neighborhoods in Southern Shores overlap with neophyte developments—Ocean Crest and Bias Shores—still taking shape along the southern tip of Duck.

"Back in the '60s," Stick says, "I would take the whole family, load them in my Jeep station wagon, and head north. We'd go through Duck, but we'd go on beyond there to the really nice beaches, because the beach in Duck had never been very good. There were too many high sand hills, and the beach sand was too coarse. I don't know what they've done to it now, but at that time, Corolla had much finer sand, much better beaches."

Though the beaches in today's Duck hardly seem substandard, it is simple to envision the challenge involved in navigating the terrain before paths were cut, cleared, and paved. Duck, though one of the narrowest sections of the Outer Banks, is remarkably hilly. Its lowest points bordering the Currituck Sound, the village rises in a series of uneven sand peaks until it slopes, rather steeply, at the beachfront. Thick underbrush continues to flourish on the numerous dunes that remain. Sand spurs, twisted catbrier, thick bayberry, and dense salt-meadow hay, though helping to protect and anchor these dunes, make hiking over them prickly and precarious.

❧ ❧ ❧

Stick's stories can pull a listener into the past. Years roll back, but the sun keeps moving forward. Now, the brilliance of high noon is a memory. Yellow light no longer illuminates Stick's living room, and the bay, rippling at midday, has flattened out across its banks. Shadows dim the ceiling and dust the walls. They shade Frank Stick's paintings. A dusky curve crowns the head of an anxious hound and makes him look all the hungrier. The same effect softens the arched back of a leaping bluefish. Foretelling the onset of winter's early nightfall, the sky shows gray in the spaces between thin, milky clouds. Stick talks about the time when things started changing in Duck.

"Sometime in the early or mid-'50s," he says, "I was living in Colington, and a group of local men, most of whom had been in the Coast Guard and had either bought or inherited property up in that area, were concerned about determining what they owned. At that point, a deed would say something like, 'Beginning at a stake on the sound side' and then possibly identify it [the piece of property] as being 'one hundred feet north of the northwest corner of the Tom King house, proceeding then in an easterly direction to the Atlantic Ocean.' That was about all the information they had, and they wanted something more accurate.

"I was asked to go up to Duck and help identify property boundary lines. I guess I'd say that's when I knew something was about to change up there—when people began worrying about how much of that land was theirs."

Stick pauses, as if to weigh the accuracy of what he just said. Then, with a nod, he remembers a map he once drew of Duck. He heads upstairs to find it. In the loft that serves as his office, past and present merge on bookshelves and worktables situated around the edges of the room. A fax and a copy machine share space with a small library of antique books, mostly atlases. Labeled boxes filled with notes and correspondence are stacked neatly against the walls, while four-foot-wide metal filing drawers, filled with land surveys and maps of various sizes, form a partition along the left side of the room.

After opening a half-door in the middle of the longest wall, Stick ducks and peeks inside a storage closet. His voice is muffled. "I think the map's in here," he says before disappearing.

An old calendar lies on a long worktable. A Virginia oil company's first attempt at marketing, this customer gift bears an image of a hunter and a hound. The artist's style is recognizable, even though Frank Stick's work has been shrunk to fit nicely into the space between the company's name and the January page.

Stick comes out of the inner room empty-handed. "Not in there," he says. He pushes a stack of boxes aside and begins opening the metal filing-cabinet drawers, explaining that he is still in the process of coding all his research material. On his third try, in a low drawer, he looks determinedly. "Here it is. Yes, this is it."

At the copy machine, Stick places the map on the glass. "Let's see what we get this way." He examines the first copy closely. When he determines that a small section of the original is missing, he slides the legal-sized sheet forward, tries it a second time. "I'm a perfectionist," he says. Stick hands over a copy of his carefully drawn map, still warm from the machine.

Near the bottom of the stairs, framed and mounted

on the wall, two parchment certificates hang side by side. The raised seal of the University of North Carolina is on one. They praise Stick for his scholarship, his dedication to researching North Carolina's history and helping to educate the public about its culture; they mention his numerous books published by the University of North Carolina Press, his philanthropic pursuits. "Oh," Stick says, "that's my Distinguished Alumnus Award."

Never having gone back to college after he "flunked out" of the university, Stick is now honored as one of the school's most notable scholars. No stranger to acknowledgments of his work, Stick won the Brown-Hudson Folklore Award, given to "persons who have in special ways contributed to the appreciation, continuation, or study of North Carolina traditions," in 1989. But recognition by the university speaks of something greater than one man's accomplishments. When David Stick came to the Outer Banks, he embraced the Dare County way of doing things, the methods that break with tradition and separate the county from the mainland. This maverick quality has its own history, beginning with the people whose resourcefulness and resilience allowed them to endure and flourish despite the harsh environment, the changing economics, and the isolation of Outer Banks living. Never bowing to protocol, Dare County residents have always known that their small, widely separated communities are different and that, as a result, their lives don't readily comply with mainlanders' prescriptions for success. Risk takers like the generations before them, Dare residents have yearnings for making their own way, forging their own path.

Stick has fashioned a life dictated by passions: for the Outer Banks, for Dare County, for uncovering all the layers until he reaches bottom and can see where it all began. His work gives testimony to perseverance, to holding one's breath, to diving way down deep and surfacing with a handful of grit, yet finding in it the tiniest treasure. Stick looks at the award, a semi-smile on his face, a sign of humble satisfaction in the university's appreciation for his work and its value, its highest praise for a man and his Dare County style.

❧ ❧ ❧

I dig for my car keys, standing with Stick on the steps outside. He sends me on my way with an old map of Duck and some reminders, his last words filling the space between us. "Good luck," he says.

A few minutes later, in the parking lot of a pizzeria in Kitty Hawk, I flip on the car's interior light to glance briefly at the hand-drawn map Stick copied. From north to south are twenty-five tracts of land, rectangles stacked like boxes between ocean and sound, gold mines once Duck's development began. On closer inspection, at what is now the northern tip of Duck's commercial area, I find the largest parcel—921 feet, more than three football fields of property running from sea to sound. It belonged to Amy Wright. Duck had only two postmasters. Amy was the second, succeeding Lloyd Toler to operate the village's mail service from 1911 until the Duck post office closed in 1941. I wonder for what price Amy would have sold out; I wonder what her heirs may have gotten for their shares.

By Stick's account, Duck saw little growth during the first half of the twentieth century. Scanning the map, I perform a quick head count, itemizing the parcels marked with the same family names. Two parcels totaling more than 1,000 feet belonged to Scarboroughs. The three parcels owned by the Wards encompassed 1,282 feet, interrupted by a 412-foot section belonging to C. A. Woodhouse. Two parcels bore the name Tillett. In the mid-1950s, the village of Duck essentially belonged to twenty-one families.

Driving north along N.C. 12, I pass through Southern Shores. Its palatial oceanfront houses and high, wide wall of dunes stand like monuments to Frank Stick and a plan come to fruition. A growing Atlantic wind rattles the car window. Its force is another reminder of how nature, too, has a plan, a determined course for the Outer Banks that pushes them every minute and ever so gently closer to the mainland.

Clouds move in from the east. Tomorrow, they will linger over the sand, drench the dunes in a chilling rain. Maybe it was a stretch of gray October sky or the cold-hearted dimness of a February morning that first made me so curious about this place. It is always in nature's cheerlessness that I think about the earliest Bankers, the ones who settled what is now Duck and the other towns in Dare County. I wonder how much courage this thin strip of sand can hold, how much it has already sapped over the years from the people who willingly risked it all on a chance as unsure as this wind-swept barrier island.

When those old-time Bankers passed on, they had no idea how valuable their sons' and daughters' inheritances would become. Even a thousand feet of water-front property held no guarantee. There were never any sure bets here. Maybe the greatest virtue of this place has nothing to do with its ocean-view houses or sound-front lots, but with longings so intense they can't be shaken, blown off, or washed away. Maybe the Bankers' greatest bequest was their ability to be dreamers, to hold firm despite all the challenges and uncertainties, to abide.

It's the salt spray, I've been told, that can stunt the growth of plants along the Atlantic beachfront. On the Outer Banks, the habitat is too brutal for much of nature's greenery. But panic grass, sea elder, and evening primrose flourish on the frontal dunes in Duck. They know how to survive the harsh winds, the blowing sand, the shifts and changes that mark these shores. Dune plants thrive and spread because their roots grow down, then out. They dig deep. Maybe that is the legacy nature has left to the Bankers, old and new. It's a lesson that even the outsiders who have decided to stay, like David Stick, seem to have learned.

Bygone days may have proven that nothing comes easily to those who seek beginnings on the Outer Banks. Yet when I'm here, all of the effort makes sense. The beauty, the mystery, the stories of aviators and dune builders, the adventures of dodging smoke bombs or digging for them under a sliver of white moon—all seem reason enough to hope that in this place, almost anything is possible.

No longer is it hard imagining what the Duck of the 1950s must have looked like—just a drowsy village with twenty-one property owners, one store, and probably fewer than a hundred residents. Approaching Duck Blind Villas, my car has sole possession of the road. Nothing moves in front of or behind me. It's nearly suppertime in the off-season, and Duck lulls. Only the faint pink glow of a sinking sun lingers over the Currituck. Streetlights will click on soon, but they haven't sensed night's coming yet.

It seems I could almost be driving into Duck's past. I envision the old village. The road is something other than smooth, black tar. I feel mounds of graded sand beneath the tires. The curves sharper and coming more quickly, I slow down, expecting rough spots ahead.

Dozens of wild ducks streak a steel-gray sky. On the Currituck, a few hunters patch blinds with pine brush or pole their skiffs homeward through the shallow sound. On a front porch, neighborhood women spread a fishing net over their laps, their song a psalm for Sunday's service, their hands busy mending for the next day's catch. To the right and left, groves of oak grow without interruption. Their branches are bent and partially stripped of leaves. Like old sentries, they wave me in through the winter dusk.

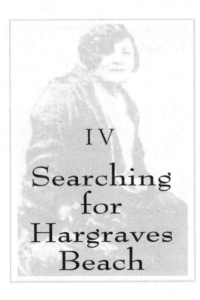

IV

Searching for Hargraves Beach

Too bad dead men tell no tales. If they did, it's likely Henry Hargraves would have already stirred from his resting spot in Elizabeth City's Oak Grove Cemetery. I would have preferred letting him narrate this story about Duck himself.

Truth is, the full measure of Henry's life has been lost to time. Like so many fine points eroded by the years, just about every secret and subtlety was laid to rest with him over three decades ago. What remains are flickers and glimmers: some part of Henry dwells in the memories of those few old enough to remember him; some part rises like an echo from the land he once owned and the buildings he once occupied. On the obituary page of a local paper, the entirety of Henry's days amounts to a respectful three paragraphs. Filed away are a handful of documents with his name on them: Dare and Pasquotank County deeds itemize what he bought, leased, sold. State certificates verify his birth and death. It is a lifetime reduced to vital statistics and the impersonal language of law.

Only a single reminder of Henry's presence on the North Banks survives: the *1998 Beach Book*, an Outer Banks telephone directory, lists eighty-two streets in Duck. Among them is Hargraves Street, though neither a current map nor a slow ride through the village reveals any such place. Searching out the specifics of Henry's life is like raking Duck for the road that once bore his name. His is a visage from the past, a story full of twists and turns, starts and stops, detours and dead ends. This rendering seeks authenticity, though it is not factual in the purest sense. It includes both certainties and speculations; it is tethered to what can be known and buoyed by what can only be imagined.

❦❦❦

If Henry were to tell it, he'd probably begin on Clinton Street in Petersburg, Virginia, where he was born in the heat of July 1891. The son of a cart man, Henry might explain how he grew up poor but plucky, how he overcame many hardships, even made it to college, studying at North Carolina's Shaw University for a short time, then deciding it was a trade and not a teaching career he wanted. He'd likely smile about his foresight and the choices he made: his decision to settle in Elizabeth City; his courting of Rosa White, one of the prettiest and most popular women in town; his marrying her and achieving middle-class comfort. He'd

HENRY HARGRAVES MARRIED ROSA WHITE, ONE OF THE PRETTIEST AND MOST POPULAR WOMEN IN ELIZABETH CITY. THIS PHOTOGRAPH OF ROSA CAME FROM HER OBITUARY IN THE LOCAL NEWSPAPER.
Courtesy of the Kirn Library, Norfolk, Virginia

likely recall how he amassed financial security while Rosa attracted too many friends to name.

He'd also account for the dream that led him to an isolated tract of North Banks land—a parcel on the outskirts of a village the locals called Duck, dozens of sandy acres overgrown with scrub oak and evening primrose, salt-meadow hay and cordgrass, pine and yaupon. He'd point out the area he purchased with his friends John Henry Bias and Charles Jenkins just months before the Great Depression. He'd describe his portion of that acreage as being golden as a summer sunrise.

Color is something Henry certainly would have understood. Growing up in the South at the turn of the twentieth century, he would have recognized how little it took to induce prejudice in an ivory-coated nation. Nothing—not a man's demeanor, work ethic, or wisdom—was powerful enough to transcend his race. The pigment of skin, the width of a nose, the thickness of lips, the texture of hair—these features decreed the character of black Americans long after the Emancipation Proclamation proclaimed them free. Henry, though fair-skinned, had slave-ship ancestry. A popular barber with dozens of white customers, he knew what it meant to be a black man.

Perhaps Henry believed that resolve and patience would eventually lead to equality. Like many blacks of the era, he may have devised his own sort of prohibition by the 1920s: with a constant smile implying contentment, they concealed whatever blues and bitterness they felt as cleverly as bootleggers hid their liquor. Adept as he may have been at averting the biases that plagued those years, Henry might loosen the fetters of the Jim Crow South, but he could never escape them.

Compared with their neighbors in other Southern states, white North Carolinians prided themselves as moderates during Reconstruction. Yet for most blacks, the racial harmony credited to their state in the early decades of the twentieth century probably seemed little more than political propaganda. There was no denying the signs that separated "Colored" from "White," no ignoring the message that Negroes were just fine as long as they remembered their place.

In Elizabeth City, life went along peacefully. Since neighborhoods and schools were divided by color, whites could keep Negroes at a comfortable distance. Even a man like Henry couldn't obliterate this reality: he wasn't welcome to share a meal with, buy his shoes from, live on the same street as, or raise his voice in prayer with the white men who frequented his shop, the same men who waited for a trim in the swivel chairs, the same men who brought their squirmy, peach-and-cream-faced boys to him for their first haircut, the same men who closed their eyes and stretched their necks, trusting that Henry would shave them close and clean with a steady hand and a freshly sharpened straight razor.

Over the years, Henry watched many of his people migrate north. Kin and neighbors packed up and moved away, expecting to leave behind the low wages and long hours of tenant farming, the meager opportunities, the shriveled hopes of advancing prosperity. They yearned for a voice in their government and a chance at the future that the Constitution guaranteed. They knew their children would need shoes with sturdier soles and wool coats with quilted linings, but the harder winters of New York and Chicago promised finer schools, new books to read, a chance to vote.

In a tattered era with a twisted righteousness, Henry stayed below the Mason-Dixon line, clipping and grooming, making polite conversation with his white clientele, imagining just how sweet real justice might someday taste. By all accounts, he was a steady church-goer and a generous contributor, a conscientious neighbor who played an integral role in Elizabeth City's black community. Tall, broad shouldered, with an athletic physique and skin like caramel cream, Henry had eyes as warm and brown as roasted chestnuts. His wavy, dark hair was prematurely streaked with gray. He polished those natural good looks with equal measures of moxie and benevolence, a memorable mix of grit and grace.

Recalling Henry as confident but never boastful, proud but never vain, folks credit him as being a wise spender with a natural instinct for business and a personal code of ethics. He knew the difference between what he liked—home-cooked meals and hand-tailored clothes, good-looking women and good times—and what he needed. Rumors are that Henry may have bent a few laws and put an ache in a few women's hearts. But no one accuses him of breaking anything. Friends and acquaintances remember not a perfect man but a decent one, a likable guy.

For Henry, Rosa's love and music seemed every bit as good as religion. She was his grace, jazz and blues his sacraments. He might find red-hot absolution in a trumpeter's improvisation, take communion in the soulful wail of a sax. There was healing power in the old-timers' field songs, holy redemption in Negro spirituals.

Henry was a dreamer. One vision drew him to the North Banks. Decades before Americans heard the riveting speeches of Martin Luther King, Jr., Henry was already imagining a promised land. His would be a respite, a way station where the burdened could let down their heavy loads, a place where the wind treated everything and everyone with equal force or equal tenderness, a refuge where nature was as blind as the newly born. There, pleasure would know no color, and freedom would flow as easily as air. What came ashore for whites would come ashore for blacks, the same waves washing the feet of every man, woman, and child who stood along the strand.

For Henry, buying land in Duck seemed the most

sage of all his investments. He would gladly hand over whatever amount of cash it took for a share of those barren dunes and marshes. With Charles Jenkins and John Bias, he purchased a piece of the promised land.

❧ ❧ ❧

The sign reads "Bias Shores." Facing Duck Road is an artistically designed concrete triangle that shares a small island with two spotlights and a rainbow of petunias. An impressive welcome, it marks the entrance to one of the village's more recent and imposing sea-to-sound subdivisions.

In the distance, Priscilla Bias's beachfront home rises like a towering sand structure, three stories of fine-grained stucco packed smooth and stained a pale coral. Decks wind around the back and stretch along both sides of the upper levels. Beyond the glass doors of a third-floor living room, yards of wood planking shadow the dunes and lead to the Atlantic. A satellite dish anchored to the roof looks as if it might catch the passing clouds.

Fiddling with the straps of their pink and yellow bikini tops, three small girls peek over the railing at the newcomers who mount the steps. One smiles; another says hello; the littlest hides behind a towel. They go back to their play—an unnamed game, a combination of hopscotch, giggles, and hide-and-seek—on the second-level deck. Their busy feet don't seem to bother a dozing beige mutt; still damp from its run on the

TODAY, PRISCILLA BIAS'S BEACHFRONT HOME RISES LIKE A TOWERING
SAND STRUCTURE ON THE LAND.
Courtesy of Peter J. Mercier, III

beach, the dog lies splayed across the landing like a worn
rug.

On most weekends, Priscilla's house stretches to
accommodate family and friends. Today, a Sunday,
they're inside sipping cool drinks from tall glasses, soak-
ing up the music and laughter that underscore pockets
of animated conversation, an amiable debate about local politics, an analysis of college basketball and the
upcoming season. Octogenarians in go-to-meeting finery and teenagers in sweats and bathing suits—all are
welcome to sit on a Queen Anne sofa and love seat, the
Chippendale chairs.

"When I built down here," Priscilla says, running
her hand over the green-and-blue brocade, "I didn't buy

beach furniture. I just brought my things from home."

Home was Scotland Neck in Halifax County, where Priscilla spent more than half her life. In addition to taking care of an often-ailing husband and raising two sons, she taught sixth grade there for forty-one years. A self-described nurturer, Priscilla has been tending to folks and rearing children, whether her own or somebody else's, for as long as she can remember.

Now matriarch of the family in Duck and a recent widow, Priscilla is anything but alone. Four generations of Biases share this house. Son Francis moved to Duck from Detroit after retiring as a veterinarian for the government. Grandson Steve, Francis's son, an electrician, lives here, as does grandson J. C., the grown child of Priscilla's other son, John. The little girls playing on the deck below are Priscilla's great-granddaughters. Longtime family friend Leola Morgan, an eighty-year-old retired teacher and former councilwoman, has come from Elizabeth City for an afternoon visit, and one of Priscilla's former students is staying with her while he refinishes the kitchen floor.

Born in 1909, Priscilla lived in Washington, D.C., and attended Howard University. There, she met John Calvin Bias.

"I married him while we were still in school," she says. "I was studying science, math, and elementary education. After we finished college, we moved to North Carolina, and I started teaching. My husband taught for a time. Then he became a principal. We were both edu-cators until we retired. We were together sixty-eight years."

In eastern North Carolina, educational advancement for blacks and the name Bias go hand in hand. John Henry Bias, Priscilla's father-in-law, became the first president of Elizabeth City State Normal School, now Elizabeth City State University, on May 25, 1928. He and his wife, Frances Lane Bias, had already dedicated many years to instilling students with their love of learn-ing. They believed that the future depended on unfaltering integrity and faith, good works and well-trained minds.

PRISCILLA (SECOND FROM LEFT) AND JOHN CALVIN BIAS (FAR RIGHT) PICTURED AT 1960 COMMENCEMENT CEREMONY AT ELIZABETH CITY STATE UNIVERSITY.
Courtesy of Elizabeth City State University Archives

"My husband's father," Priscilla says, "sent his wife once a month from Elizabeth City to Manteo to teach the children how to mend fishing nets and how to read."

"Yes, Lord," Leola adds. "And she had seven children of her own, too."

"Granddaddy sent her," Francis explains, "because, back then, they had no schools for black children down here. It wasn't until they built the college in Elizabeth City that there was any place to train black teachers in eastern Carolina."

Like his wife, John Henry Bias lived what he preached. Having secured degrees from Lincoln University, a Negro college in Missouri, he traveled north. Accepted into graduate school at the University of Chicago, he studied math and science. After that, he continued his training in educational administration and supervision at New York's Columbia University. A professor long before he was a president, Bias wanted to give back what he had received. He taught math at Lincoln, natural science at Shaw, both subjects at Elizabeth City. Speaking to faculty and students just days after being named president, Bias summarized the scope of his mission: "I am in favor of a type of education," he said, "that leads to complete living, which includes an education of the Head, Hand, and Heart."

Henry Hargraves likely appreciated Bias's philosophy, especially the part about "complete living," which, for Henry, included the pleasures every man and woman deserved after a week of hard work. While Bias groomed the minds of young blacks in classrooms across town, Henry groomed the heads of Elizabeth City's white businessmen, his stream of regular customers swelling like the nearby Pasquotank River. By the end of 1922, Henry saved enough money to buy a lot on Speed Street. Then came the house he'd planned for himself and Rosa, an impressive, two-story American Foursquare with fancy truss gables, sturdy Doric pillars, a wide porch wrapping around the front, and two more lattice porches, stacked like tiers of white wedding cake, for the back.

"They were friends," Priscilla says, "Henry and my

HENRY AND ROSA HARGRAVES BUILT THIS TWO-STORY AMERICAN FOURSQUARE HOME ON SPEED STREET IN ELIZABETH CITY.
Courtesy of Museum of the Albemarle

father-in-law. That's how they came to own this land. Seems someone owed Henry some money back in the '20s, and when he got it, he knew what he wanted, to buy down here. He'd already picked out the land. Charles Jenkins, he took care of all the buildings at the college in Elizabeth City. He decided to go in with them, too. The three of them each put in a share, and one day, I'm not sure exactly when, they had enough money to buy it."

Deeds verify that Charles Jenkins, John Henry Bias, and Henry Hargraves purchased more than eighty acres of North Banks land on April 18, 1929, a Thursday almost two weeks past Easter. It was a chilly dawn, the sky matted with storm clouds left from the night before. Within the first hours of daylight, the rain dried and the air warmed.

I imagine the details and the words of that morning, the streets filling with people, the sun growing round and yellow like the daisies Rosa Hargraves keeps in a vase on her dressing table. Henry plucks one out, clips off a section of flower and stem, and threads it through his lapel. He folds a beige linen handkerchief and tucks it into his breast pocket.

"What do you think?" he asks.

Rosa is fastening a cameo to her collar. The skin on her neck is the color of rain-soaked sand, her eyes soft and calm as the Currituck before sunrise, her hair thick like black needlerush on the high marshes. She turns around, first straightening the seams in her stockings, then glancing up at Henry. "You're a fine sight, Henry Hargraves. Look like a man ready to do a little business," she says. "I especially like that daisy."

Rosa bends over her desk, collects her books and papers. Henry admires the curve of her hips, the lengths of thigh and calf, the delicate ankles. He's thinking that a lucky man should be patient, that in another few weeks they'll be taking final exams at Roanoke Institute, the high school where Rosa teaches etiquette, home economics, and health. And then summer, the bright days and balmy nights, the fragrance of magnolias and the whirl of fans, a vacationing wife to keep out past midnight and in bed until noon. He'll close the barbershop for a week or two, take Rosa someplace special. At Christmas, she talked about a train trip and a week in New York, but he can't imagine any evening skyline finer than the one he has found over the Currituck, the sunset sweet as orange sherbet, a grinning moon, stars so bright they could be a legion of angels just waiting to open the gates of heaven.

Though they've been married more than a decade, there have been no offspring, no sons for Henry, no babies for Rosa to nurse. Her students take the place of children, and Rosa does her share of mothering in classrooms and hallways. She counsels the girls about good posture and bad manners, about caring for their teeth and skin, about genteel conversation. She shows

John Henry Bias
Courtesy of Elizabeth City State University Archives

Charles Jenkins, John Henry Bias, and Henry Hargraves purchased more than eighty acres of North Banks land on April 18, 1929 and began Hargraves Beach. Unfortunately, no photographs of Hargraves are available.

CHARLES JENKINS
Courtesy of Elizabeth City State University Archives

them how to season a tough porkchop tender, how to roll the crust for a sweet potato pie, how to make lard taste like butter. She explains how to take stains out of tablecloths and pains out of bee stings with the same mixture of cider vinegar and baking soda. She teaches them about bathing babies and disinfecting just about anything, about canning pole beans and putting up sour-cherry preserves, about starching and dyeing cotton. She helps them plan a balanced meal, hem curtains, look for a bargain, patch pockets, darn holes in their daddies' socks, sew bottons on blouses for their mothers. When they ask, Rosa advises them about curtailing the advances of fast-talking boys who make love sound as simple as a night behind the woodshed.

Young men receive instructions about grooming and hygiene. Rosa plans lessons about sterilizing milk pails, smoking hams, butchering chickens. She makes every boy pick up his feet, lift his shoulders, walk with his head held high. She demonstrates the firm squeeze he needs for shaking another man's hand and the gentler touch he should use for greeting a lady. She feels comfortable prodding the boys to keep their thoughts noble, their diction clear, and their shirttails tucked in, but the headier topics she assigns to their coaches.

The 1920s, Rosa regularly reminds Henry, are the reason she spends so many hours at Roanoke Institute. "I work overtime," she says, "because teaching them just isn't enough these days. You've got to help raise them, too. Some of my pupils, old as they are, don't seem to know the difference between right and wrong. Oh, they can read and write just fine, but no child grows straight on his own. I have to teach each one something different. Some need to learn how to be God-fearing. Others need to learn to be strong. The vain ones, I tell them that false pride is no pride at all. And I let the timid ones know they can be something, make good lives for themselves."

Henry considers that had his wife not been a teacher, she might have taken up sermonizing. Sometimes, she sounds a little too much like Dr. Cartwright and the Reverend McRay at the Cornerstone Baptist Church, where Rosa sings in the choir and Henry reaches deep into his pockets before passing the collection basket.

"These days," she likes to say, "no might as well mean yes. Lord knows, Henry, it's Prohibition, and even church folks are stilling their own liquor or paying good money to bootleggers. Can't imagine drinking anything that vile. Devils' brew, that's what the Scripture says. It's unhealthy, too. Folks say that stuff can kill a man or leave him blind."

Henry might offer Rosa the courtesy of a nod, even give her an affirmative grin, but he never says a word. He counts himself among the decent men, but he doesn't agree with every right and wrong itemized in Sunday sermons, doesn't always like being preached to.

And long ago, when he decided what real love meant, when he knew he felt it for Rosa as sure as his own heart beat, he didn't think it required his always having to see the world through her eyes. Henry can't warrant what sin there is in a man's wanting a little liquid pleasure. He can find no harm in a sip of back-room gin or cellar-bottled whiskey every now and then. Just what evil has a man committed when he puts an honestly earned five cents on the counter after a long day of farming or hauling lumber in exchange for a nickel-nip's worth of relief?

But Henry never minds Rosa's orations. Sometimes, he encourages them. He likes watching her, can't help but stare. With each word, she radiates heat, with every sentence intensity. In her face is some new beauty that only fire and brimstone give it.

"And I can just imagine what you're grinning about, Henry," Rosa sometimes says, then lowers her eyes and purses her lips, gives him a sideways glance and a half-smile. He will listen to a whole year of her sermons for just that look, his wife's secret language, her unspoken "I love you."

At the front door, Rosa gives Henry another quick inspection, smoothing back his hair the way she likes it, checking to see her reflection in the gloss of his shoes. Balanced on her toes, she stretches up to kiss his cheek. "Good luck," she says. Then she leans forward and leaves

Henry with a trace of herself—the tint of her lipstick on his lips, the scent of gardenias, her perfume, on his neck. "Say hello to John and Charles for me, and don't stay away too late tonight, you hear?"

A fresh wind, just as the newspaper forecasts, greets Henry as he leaves the house on Speed Street. A few blocks north, he turns the corner, smells breakfasts already cooked and waiting to be eaten—fried eggs, boiled grits, bitter coffee, flapjacks soaked in honey. Beating dust from rag rugs or sweeping yellow pollen from front porches, the women holler their gossip. The yards are narrow, the houses close, the fences low and crooked. When the women see Henry coming, they soften their voices. They pat down their hair, drop their brooms behind them.

Henry smiles. "Morning, ladies."

"Mornin', honey," one says.

"Mornin', handsome."

"Mornin', sweetheart."

Henry approaches 404 Ehringhaus Street, a deep, narrow, two-story building that reaches back nearly a block into the alley. It is his latest business venture. Since it has sufficient space for leasing the upstairs to Harvey's Shoe Shine Shop and Frank Carter's Clean and Press, he figures he can wring out enough rental income to cover most of the monthly mortgage payment and keep the first floor for himself. Over the months, he's worked on the plans and figured out the costs while Rosa graded essays on clean living or sewed costumes for the senior-class play, *Mammy's Little Rose*.

Henry doesn't want to waste his time on any barrel house or gyp joint. He's heard about the wine rooms Negroes have begun opening in cities up north, places that combine a billiard hall with a club room, where local musicians come to play ragtime and blues, where colored folks dance all night long. He's started collecting every record the King Oliver Jazz Band has made, played Louis Armstrong's first solo hit, "Chimes Blues," until he's almost worn it out, listened to Edward Kennedy Ellington, the man they called "Duke," and his orchestra on the radio, the broadcast coming all the way from Harlem's Cotton Club, where the best black jazzmen perform under the glow of purple lamps.

Soon, Henry plans to begin hiring men who know what to do with a saw and hammer, young men with big families or old men with big debts who need the extra work. When the remodeling begins, he will supervise every detail, picking out pine risers for a bandstand, tiger oak for the bar, pastel paints for the walls, good wood shingles and shutters. He will order tinted lights for dancing slow and close, brighter lights for high illumination, as folks will want to watch the flying fingers of a piano man or the strain of a sax player when he blows a solo so low-down his horn almost sizzles. Henry will buy round tables and every color of cloth to cover them, stools for resting awhile, pool tables lined with smooth, green felt, dozens of cue sticks, and cases of glossy balls. On top of the bar, he will stack glasses and line up pitchers for sweet tea and fresh-squeezed lemonade. If he has any liquor, he won't leave it out for inspection, but rather tuck it behind the bottles of Coke and Nehi soda.

When it comes time to celebrate the grand opening, Henry will be proud to introduce Elizabeth City's black community to its own wine room—a pool parlor on one side and a dance club on the other—every bit as nice as any above the Mason-Dixon line. Henry will call it the Blue Duck Inn. Within months, he'll no longer be known simply as a white man's barber who shares a shop in the Flora Building with Ellis Alexander. In becoming a proprietor, Henry will attract another clientele, give his own people something they are sure to need—good times and good music. The Blue Duck Inn, he feels certain, will become the most popular nightspot in Elizabeth City.

But today's business is different. Henry walks a little faster. He's already kept the other men waiting, and he knows they won't let him forget it.

"Morning, Henry," John Bias says. "Thought you'd forgotten about us."

Charles Jenkins teases. "Lord knows, Henry, you forget about today? You know, this man can't get down the street without stopping to chat with the ladies. Can't help being late when he's looking so fine, suit like fresh cream, daisy in his lapel, pocket full of cash. Women always on him like flies on beet sugar. Is that lipstick on your cheek, Henry?"

They share a bench outside the Pasquotank County Courthouse. While waiting, Bias has started reviewing literature about the "Live at Home Program." A dozen bulletins from the North Carolina Department of Education lie in the open briefcase on his lap.

"Man's always working," Jenkins says of Bias as he opens a copy of the *Daily Advance*, the city's white newspaper, and scans the headlines. "I guess being a president is never easy. Even Hoover's got his share of worries. Congress fussin' about farm bills and problems with immigration."

"Charles," Henry moans, "you ever learned about reading to yourself?"

Closer to home, Jenkins finds out that fire has almost destroyed a city lumbermill, doing thirty-five thousand dollars' worth of damage and putting twenty-three men out of work. He examines the pictures of four white students from Elizabeth City High School's debating team who have left for Chapel Hill to compete in the State Forensic Championship. Out-of-town evangelists are attracting record crowds at the local white churches, preaching about evil, about selling one's salvation, about the diamond that is a white man's soul.

Henry scans the latest edition of the race-record

catalog from Columbia Records. He counts the new releases he's already heard—"Tell Me When" and "Empty House Blues" by Clara Smith, "Hope I'll Join the Band" by the Birmingham Jubilee Singers, and Coley Jones's "I Used to Call Her Baby" and "Chasin' Rainbows."

The Harris family goes inside the courthouse first. It's their land in Duck that Hargraves, Bias, and Jenkins have bid on, most of it property the Harrises either inherited or purchased from the Vickers clan for next to nothing at the turn of the century, land they probably never expected they would one day turn over to blacks. But money is money, and in 1929, available acreage in a remote North Banks village like Duck doesn't attract many takers.

By noon, all parties are satisfied, having exchanged twenty-one hundred dollars in cash for eighty-four acres, the deed witnessed, signed, and notarized by the county clerk, Miss Helen Turner. The deal officially closed, the sellers leave the building without smiles, conversation, or handshakes.

On September 20, 1930, Bias, Jenkins, and Hargraves return to the Pasquotank County Courthouse to divide their purchase into three parts. Each one takes a section running from ocean to sound.

"Got fishing at dawn and crabbing at dusk," Henry had told them. They remember his sales pitch and how they hadn't needed much coaxing after he took them to see the place.

They have already agreed that the size of each man's portion will depend on the amount of his investment. Jenkins chooses the northern piece, 570 feet of ocean-front. Bias opts for the middle, 445 feet along the Atlantic. Henry gets what he wants, the southern tip and 572 feet of shoreline.

❧ ❧ ❧

Priscilla Bias closes her eyes as if something pains her. She's thinking about how to describe the past. "After Henry, Mr. Jenkins, and my father-in-law split up the land," she says, "we started coming down here. It was in the '30s, and we came by barge. Nobody would sell us anything. We couldn't even buy a glass of water around Manteo. We'd have to go south of there, where the white people were different. They'd remember us from one time to the next, and they never refused us, always sold us gas and sodas.

"Of course, there wasn't any road like there is now. To get up this far, you'd have to let some air out of two tires and drive real slow on the sand along the sound. We'd pass by Henry's land first. Then we'd get up to right about where we are now. We could walk straight across from the sound to the beach. We'd just come for the day, crab and fish, and then go back home. Course, back then, we had no place of our own to stay for the night, and we couldn't get a room in the white hotels around Nags Head. Sometimes, we'd see a few people from the village. They'd be down here on my father-in-law's property fishing."

The 1930s brought some cruel years. For John Bias and Charles Jenkins, it was a decade of challenge. For Henry, it was the best and worst of times, his gains almost sublime, his losses the sort that can never be recovered. The Great Depression put a strain on the entire nation, the South's plight so severe President Roosevelt declared it the country's "number one economic problem." Poor whites traded low-paying farm jobs for low-paying mill jobs. Poor blacks, not having much opportunity to make such an exchange, stayed on the land. Even after the government started sending subsidies to assist the struggling rural communities, black tenant farmers and lumbermen saw their wages steadily shrink.

In Elizabeth City, Henry gave up being a barber after the Flora Building burned to the ground in 1930. Instead of cutting hair, he managed the building on Ehringhaus Street and opened the doors of the Blue Duck Inn, where every local out-of-work man was welcome to spend his afternoons playing pool or hands of pitty-pat. Weekend evenings, the music drew crowds. Partners tried new dance steps, swinging each other into a joyful sweat after Henry brought Cab Calloway and his jitterbug songs to town. When there was no band, Henry played top tunes ordered from the race-record catalogs. Those rhythms were almost as intoxicating as the nickel nips of gin fewer and fewer could afford to buy. In 1933, Congress repealed Prohibition, after which Henry served every kind of beverage, hard and soft, to customers with or without ready cash.

Constantly short of funds was John Bias, who, regardless of deficits or the Depression, always managed to improve conditions at Elizabeth City State Normal School. It was his idea to initiate a barter system, which allowed even destitute students a way to finance their education by working on campus. Along walkways, students planted the flowering bushes they'd dug out of neighboring woods. Some slaughtered hogs, tended fields of butter beans and strawberries, milked cows, or churned cream into butter. Others assisted with the preparation of breakfast and dinner, serviced the dining hall, set tables with linens, china, and silver, or cleared it all away, everything washed and put back before the next meal. Faculty and administration thinned, but a core of them, including Charles Jenkins, refused to abandon their positions despite the unavoidable 50 percent pay cut. Year after year, Elizabeth City's black community watched with pride as John Bias led the procession of graduates.

Two late-summer hurricanes pummeled the North Banks in 1933. The beach and marsh were eroded by a current of seawater more than a foot deep. The wind dug gullies all over Duck, and a week's worth of heavy rain filled them. The puddles grew so wide and deep that village children used them as swimming pools until the air chilled and the sand started drying up in mid-autumn.

By then, Henry had begun making regular day trips to the North Banks. Over time, he surveyed every inch of his property in Duck, studied its contours, climbed its dunes, counted the stands of live oak and the pigs that rolled in the shade beneath them. He gave names to the mallards that camped in his marsh grass along the Currituck, tracked the circling flight of ospreys ready to nest, cleared a footpath through the woods.

After a few years, even a restless Atlantic couldn't unnerve him. It might slap his face like a churlish lover or bully him to his knees, but he grew to trust its irregular rhythms, expecting it would always lift him up and carry him safely back to shore. Henry took a liking to blowing sand and the acrid spit of the sea, to the rough and salty kisses they left on his cheeks and lips. The glaring sun was a just another big, white face, one he could look into and laugh at. He forgot about the fright in a willet's scream, and when the meadow larks stopped singing their lilting love song, Henry still heard its melody.

❧ ❧ ❧

"Henry would come here often," Priscilla says. "But I don't think Rosa came as much. After a few years, Henry decided to build a club on his land. He wanted the chauffeurs and domestics who came to Nags Head and Kitty Hawk for the summer with the white families to have a place to go for entertainment, someplace of their own."

Leola Morgan nods. "Henry had one vision. He wanted to establish a community for Negroes down here. That was his goal. That definitely became his aim in life."

Like all of Henry's visions, this one included a carefully thought-out plan. By the late 1930s, the financial burdens of the Depression were beginning to ease. The Blue Duck Inn had managed to hold its own, and rentals from the building on Ehringhaus Street had steadily brought him an income. Henry kept up with the nation's fiscal progress, with New Deal programs and the predictions of Washington economists. The coming years promised something better.

Along the shore of the barrier islands, Henry had watched dune builders at work. He had passed the National Park Service camp in Duck, had witnessed the village gladly bulge to accommodate almost a hundred new faces. He had heard rumors about the Big Apple, a makeshift shack operated by a white man named Morrisette, a rough but good-natured guy the locals called "Pork Chops," who was said to sell beer without a license.

Soon, Henry didn't seem to worry that social changes weren't following quickly enough. It would no longer matter that blacks couldn't sit on the beaches in

Nags Head and Kitty Hawk, that they were barred from the restaurants and hotels and summer dances. He could help move things along. Legally possessing a share of the Outer Banks meant Henry could control the future of his acreage. And he knew exactly what he wanted to do, had known it all along.

From Elizabeth City, Henry hired some of the same men who had helped him customize the Blue Duck Inn. He bought a used military-surplus bus, loaded it with laborers and their tools and enough supplies for a day's work. By dawn, they were headed toward the barge that would take them across the Albemarle Sound, then over miles of ungraded sand, around the pines and cedars, up the gritty mounds until four worn tires rolled past the entrance of his land.

Along the boundary line, where his property bumped up against the old route to Duck, Henry asked the workmen to erect two wide pillars. He watched as they worked, leveling the ground in the morning, sandwiching rows of red brick between layers of cement until the dim light of dusk. At quitting time, Henry led them to a balding sand hill overlooking the Currituck. A few stripped off their shoes and shirts and waded into the water while Henry spread the blanket. The rest watched as he unloaded the baskets some of Rosa's students had helped her pack that morning— plates with fried chicken and thick slices of molasses-glazed ham, bowls of cornmeal biscuits and honey for dipping, black-eyed peas and buttered corn, two fat peach pies and Henry's favorite, sweet potato pudding. They ate until their plates were empty. They helped themselves to seconds. After dessert, they passed the flasks a few carried in their pockets. Then they threw crumbs to the dozing mallards Henry treated like adopted children and watched the gulls hovering overhead. One of the men started humming. Another slapped out a rhythm with a spoon against his palm. Soon, every man joined in, a band with voices for horns and utensils for percussion.

Henry brought workers back the next week and the week after that. Some men took a wife or sweetheart along, others worn musical instruments—an old trumpet, a dented clarinet, a saxophone somebody's daddy had found on a train after the Great War, a yellowed banjo left to one of them in a white man's will. They worked, stacking the pillars high, adding more bricks and a heavy square of concrete to join them. Once the archway was completed, Henry gave them another task. They smoothed wet plaster over the concrete block, then etched two words into it: *Hargraves Beach*. By sunset, they were celebrating. This occasion warranted pints of whiskey to go along with the plates of fried chicken and the peach pie. As seabirds and waterfowl settled in the grass to nibble leftovers, each man raised his cup to Henry. Under the stars, the wives danced barefoot while their men played thin, high-flying renditions of "Tiger Rag" and Joe Oliver's "Dippermouth."

Within the year, Henry put aside enough money for other busloads of supplies. He brought the same men back to Hargraves Beach, helped them measure and calculate, then paced along the bank as they drove a dozen thick wooden posts deep into the silt bottom of the Currituck. A few feet above the shallow sound, they framed a large, square box, and Henry checked the braces on every side. Closer to the ocean, he put men to work sawing down trees and clearing a lot big enough for a two-room house, the beach cottage he'd planned for himself and Rosa, an anniversary surprise whose blueprint he'd kept locked in a skinny desk drawer.

Over the next months, Henry paid at least a dozen workers a good hourly wage to spend Saturdays on his land in Duck. On the Atlantic side, there were four men for sawing, sanding, and building the cottage; along the Currituck, there were two for cutting planks, two for wading into the sound with a fifteen-foot board between them, two for fastening each board to the box, and two for hammering one board to another; there were also two for supervising the work on both projects because Henry couldn't always be there. When they finished the elevated floor of Henry's outdoor club, it stretched from the water to the same sand hill where they had eaten and drunk and made music months before. The little cottage was beginning to take shape, already had its foundation and walls. They wanted Henry to see it.

On a late-April Saturday, Henry's workmen stood outside the Blue Duck Inn in a cold drizzle. They had stepped on to an empty bus and found no supplies, no Henry to point out this and that to the foremen, no baskets of chicken and sweet-smelling pies, no pages with scribbled instructions and carefully drawn diagrams. Nothing. Maybe Henry had heard the wind would be strong, the weather too bad for them to work. Maybe he was low on cash or he'd overslept. It seemed Henry had forgotten—about the bus, about the supplies, about the waiting workmen, about the open-air pavilion and the cottage he was building in Duck.

Henry knew something the others didn't—Rosa was dying. Months before, a local doctor had felt the lump, told her not to worry, said it probably wasn't cancer. When the specialist recommended a mastectomy, Henry had taken Rosa to Virginia, to the Parrish Memorial Hospital in Portsmouth, where another doctor took one of her breasts in surgery, then followed it up with words Henry didn't want to hear. Rosa's prognosis was grim.

Henry tried talking her into whatever experimental treatment medicine had to offer. "No," she said. "I think they've taken enough of me. I just want to go home."

By her bedside, Henry listened to the prayers Rosa whispered when an infection set in, felt his hopes rise with every hymn the congregation sang at the Cornerstone Baptist Church. He wasn't sure he believed in miracles. But if he had to, he'd bargain with his faith, make any deal God wanted if it meant keeping Rosa alive. When she pretended she was stronger, when she got out of bed each morning, when she tried to continue teaching during the days and keeping her regular schedule of church meetings and choir practices at night, Henry tried to forget that his wife had ever been ill.

But by the spring of 1938, Henry could no longer pretend that he didn't see, didn't hear. Rosa cried only when she thought he wasn't around, but she couldn't control the moaning and wincing in her sleep. The pain started out like sparks: a pinch between her shoulders, a jab in her neck, a poke in her head, her arms and legs first stiff, then numb and heavy as anvils, a burning in the base of her back like somebody had lit the fuse on a stick of dynamite. She made Henry promise that he would not force her to lie in another hospital bed until she had finished out the school year.

"And we'll pray," she said.

It's a cool June morning, raindrops from the night's storm still rolling down the windows. Henry puts another nightgown in Rosa's suitcase. The doctors have told him she'll be there a long time, as long as it takes, maybe weeks or months. He sees her resting on the second-level porch, dozing in her favorite chair, the oak rocker he gave her on her last birthday, her forty-third. It is the one piece of furniture she's comfortable in, the only one she sleeps in. Henry knew right away he'd buy it, thought it must have been made for Rosa, a chair with crocheted daisies on the cushioned seat and back.

He doesn't want to wake her; he'd like to lift her up and carry her to their bed, slide her between the soft, clean sheets and lie next to her, protect her, make her God listen to reason, yell at his God for not giving her more time, for not making her whole again.

"Cancer eats you up, bit by bit," Rosa has told him. "Can't be helped. You know that, Henry. You've got to stop praying for what's not meant to be and start praying for what is. Ask God if I can go quick and peaceful, in my sleep, in our own house."

But Henry can't do it. He can't rely on Rosa's faith. If it won't cure her, medicine might. The doctors at Parrish Hospital are expecting Rosa. Henry needs to get her there no later than ten. He looks at the clock, at Rosa resting, at the chair, remembers her smile and what she said after he brought it up the stairs: "Nicest gift you ever gave me, Henry. Can't be thinking about dying as long as you're sitting on top of the daisies."

He decides to fold just one more nightgown. It's already past seven-thirty.

It's so hot in the Cornerstone Baptist Church that the senior choir has to fan themselves with their hymnals. Fannie Vaughan has already practiced the first two verses of "O When I Come to the End on My Journey" before Henry realizes that every pew is filled. Women are being shown to the rows of folding chairs the ushers have squeezed into the aisles. Most of the men have given up their seats and stand in alcoves or narrow corners. The Reverend McRay and Dr. Cartwright, who will soon be sharing the pulpit, are still greeting the mourners who have come to praise God for his mercy or express their condolences.

Between Henry and the pulpit is Rosa, dressed in milk-colored linen and lying on yellow satin in the open casket. He hears the women whisper as they pass the coffin and look inside:

"Face's sweet in death as it was in life."

"Cancer. I heard it came back."

"All over her, poor thing. Got into her spine."

"Stayed in that hospital for two months. Not a thing they could do for her."

"Hush. I don't care what they say about that place he runs, the man never left her bedside."

Everyone tries hard to please her. They sing her favorite hymns. Olivia Sessoms's solo of "Flee As a Bird to Your Mountain" causes the women to sob. Even some of the men are holding back tears. Henry thinks Rosa would like the messages of condolence Mr. Fleming reads, the bouquets her students have sent for the service, and the trays of food they have fixed for the reception.

With Rosa gone and the house on Speed Street empty, Henry spends most of the fall and winter grieving. Then spring comes. He puts Rosa's daisy chair next to their bed, talks out loud as if she were still sitting in it, tells her he needs air and light, that he's only and always loved her, that he is still going to church because she would want him there.

He thinks he hears her talking back, telling him that she never expected him to die along with her: *What were all those projects you were working on before I got so sick? What was all that fuss about, that big ugly bus and all those baskets filled with suppers for men I never met? Where will Negroes have to go if you're not going to make a place for them? Shouldn't they have a chance to walk barefoot in the sand, taste salt and smell pine, hear the geese and gulls, blow their horns and beat their bucket drums, watch fireworks on the Fourth of July, dance under a summer moon? What God would keep colored folks off the Outer Banks when he welcomes them into heaven?*

The next day, Henry got to work. First, he gave the bus a facelift, painted it yellow, patched the seats, polished the chrome, put on new tires. When he was finished, it looked pleasing, good enough to suit even Rosa. Then he called the workmen back to their Saturday jobs. After loading supplies and buying the laborers breakfast, he put the keys in one of the foremen's hands, told him to drive. Henry sat in the back, where the Hargraves Beach band practiced—the sultry whine of a sax, the blast of a trumpet, a twanging banjo—all the way to Duck. The men understood that from then on, whenever they rode to the Outer Banks, music would travel with them on the refurbished bus Henry called "Miss Rosa."

Before long, the beach cottage had its roof and windows, the pavilion its lattice knee-walls and railings. On weekends in good weather, Henry would find friends and the friends of friends waiting for Miss Rosa and a day trip to Duck. News of Hargraves Beach and Henry's outdoor club on the Currituck Sound spread through Elizabeth City. When it reached the Cornerstone Baptist Church, some members shook their heads in disapproval, while others twitched with anticipation. There was always plenty of good food and music, laughter carried in the wind, and the prints of dancing feet in the sand. Henry's guests swam, fished, snoozed on the beach or under the shade of a wide oak tree. By sundown, they'd be waiting on the pavilion, where fresh fish sizzled on the grills and yellow corn and blue crabs steamed in pots on a kerosene stove. Lanterns swung from the highest beams, and starlight brightened the sky.

For weeks, Henry tried convincing Dr. Cartwright

to take a ride on Miss Rosa. He promised that they'd go to Duck for an afternoon——no music or dancing on the pavilion, just a picnic on the beach, a few hours of sunshine and salt water, some inspiration for an upcoming sermon about the beauty of God's creation.

On a warm September Sunday, after the senior choir sang "Precious Lord," Cartwright stood silent at the pulpit. He saw Henry, his smile bright as a beacon, in the back of the church. The congregation was waiting. They needed a dose of their preacher's wisdom.

"You folks'll never know how it is unless I tell you," Cartwright began. "Yesterday, I went down to Hargraves Beach."

The elders in the front pews sighed; some of the women gasped out loud or fanned themselves as if to keep from fainting.

"Yes, it's true. I rode on the Miss Rosa, the bus named for our beloved sister who's already found her way through the gates of the heavenly kingdom."

"Yes, Lord."

"Amen."

"Praise God," Henry called out with the others.

"Then I joined the crowd on the beach, got myself a fine seat on that soft, warm sand. I watched the waves run up on the shore. I could see a big, broad-shouldered boy, not a face I recognized from this congregation. He was way out in the water swimming. And there was this little chippy of a girl with barely anything on. She ran out into the surf, and when one of those waves hit her, she started hollering, 'Oh, somebody help me. Lord, somebody come get me, please. I'm a-drowning.'

"Well, the Lord answered her cry for help. It was that big boy that went after her. I could see the whole thing, her slipping and squirming around and his long arms reaching in to get her. And then, Lord knows, he got her. And I can tell you, he got her good. That's the sort of thing that goes on down at Henry's. I saw it all with my own eyes. I witnessed sin on Hargraves Beach."

After the service, Henry stopped Dr. Cartwright.

"Reverend," he said, "I was wondering, who's the best contributor you have here?"

"Well, Henry, I guess that would have to be you."

"Then I'm thinking that maybe you could help me out a little with Hargraves Beach. Or maybe I should start worshiping and contributing someplace else. If that's what you want."

"No, Henry. You be sure to come back here next week."

The following Sunday, Henry decided to move closer to the pulpit. He chose a pew where spinsters and young widows sat smiling in his direction. In the year since Rosa had passed, these women's sympathies had escalated into a cooking contest for his affections—casseroles and meat pies left at his door, fruit cobblers and cherry tarts delivered in person. At almost fifty,

Henry liked thinking he could still turn a lady's head. But he figured it was his wallet as much as his features that now made them push each other over so that he could share a space among them.

Dr. Cartwright seemed nervous. He was short and round, and tiny beads of sweat clung to his forehead. He wrung his hands, paced, eyeballed the patterned rug beneath him as if he had lost a piece of his soul and expected to find it lying there. The choir hadn't yet finished the opening hymn when he mounted the pulpit. He turned to the organist and motioned for the music to stop.

"Listen to me," he said. "Before I preach today's sermon, I've got something I must say."

Henry sat up straight, raised his eyes over each head and strained neck in front of him.

"Last Sunday," Cartwright said, "I told you that I had been at Hargraves Beach. I told you what I saw there, and what I told you is as true today as it was one week ago."

Henry's eyes met Cartwright's. For a moment, it seemed as if they were both weighing the possibilities, Henry mentally counting the cash in his pocket, Cartwright imagining each one of those dollars floating out of the collection basket and following Hargraves through the door and down the street to another church.

"So what I want to say is . . ." Cartwright hesitated.

He knew he had promised Henry a good word. Then, as if God himself had unlocked his tongue, he almost shouted. "If you have to sin, go to Hargraves Beach."

❧ ❧ ❧

Francis Bias is pointing out the window in the direction of the Currituck. "Hargraves's club," he says, "used to be right over there. If you go down a ways, to that section of Ocean Crest across the street, you can still see one or two of the wood pilings sticking up out of the water."

"Henry knew how to run a business," Leola Morgan says. "He had no trouble keeping the Blue Duck Inn open for almost thirty years."

But the open-air pavilion on the Currituck lasted only a little while, maybe a year or two. It wasn't that Hargraves Beach didn't attract a crowd. It wasn't that the villagers openly objected to Henry or his business. Maybe Henry's plans to establish a black community in Duck were threatening to those who believed the Outer Banks should remain a whites-only resort. Maybe a man like Hargraves needed a warning that he should back off, move away from the land he'd rightfully bought and built on.

"They burned Henry out," Priscilla says. "We never could find out who did it, but they burned everything down, the club and the little house he'd built on the ocean side. After that, I don't think he wanted to come back as often."

In mid-July 1939, Henry lost his friend John Bias, who died in Johns Hopkins Hospital after a short illness. As a college president, Bias left Elizabeth City State Normal School considerably better off than he had found it. Under his guidance, the state granted the school permission to confer bachelor degrees in elementary education and officially changed its name to Elizabeth City State Teachers College. As a father, Bias left his children better off than they probably realized. He willed them his land in Duck.

"Each one got about seventy feet of beachfront," Priscilla says.

A decade later, Frank Stick owned the land that would eventually become Southern Shores. His property bordered Hargraves Beach on the south and was already starting to be developed. Henry had remarried. His second wife, Angelina Praro, years younger than he, was not black but Puerto Rican, a stranger to his friends in Elizabeth City.

"After they burned him out," Leola Morgan says, "I don't think Henry wanted to give up right away. He may have kept trying to get something started down here for another five or six years. But that fire, it sure slowed him down."

Tragedies can change a man, carve up his plans, cloud his vision. What Henry had created was too easily destroyed, two structures gutted by flames. To this day, the cause of the fire remains unknown. Henry probably never considered reporting it. He knew that even if he had, it would not have merited an official investigation—not a black man's property, not in a remote section of the North Banks, not fifty years ago.

Some think the fire was an act of God. A sudden bolt of lightning or a glowing ember carried on a westerly wind could have ignited the wood. Others think it may have been human error, maybe a dropped lantern spilling kerosene or a tossed cigarette smoldering in the dry grass. Some speculate it was the Klan who decided the time had come to deliver Henry a red-hot warning.

After the fire, day visitors rarely rode over the bumpy roads in Miss Rosa. The bus was put to pasture in the shade behind the Blue Duck Inn. Henry's beach house and his sound-side pavilion had been turned to ash, his dream consumed like the charred timber, all the music and laughter suffocated by smoke.

By 1950, the Sun Oil Company had come all the way from Philadelphia to lay pipes beneath the village, and the Carolina-Virginia Coastal Corporation began construction of a new road that plowed straight through Hargraves Beach. That summer, the Virginia Power Company planted poles and ran electric lines. Five years later, Henry decided it was time to start selling. By 1963, every acre of Hargraves Beach had been deeded or leased to someone.

"It was a fine dream Henry had," Leola says, "even if it never could come to fruition."

Toward the end of his life, Henry spent most days on the second-story porch sitting next to the empty oak rocker he had bought for Rosa almost thirty years before. The crocheted daisies had faded, and the flowers had just about worn away. He could hear the cars and the young people moving along Speed Street. Everything—the young men's voices, the music they listened to on their car radios—seemed a little louder than it had a generation earlier.

Henry's hearing was still finely tuned, though his once-steady hands shook and his striding gait faltered. Parkinson's disease, the doctors told him. Angelina played the old jazz records and brought Henry's meals to him on a tray. She helped him up and down the stairs until a series of small strokes made it impossible for him to do much more than wait for his young wife to turn him in bed and feed him something he wouldn't need to chew. It was a slow death.

On the evening of May 11, 1967, after a massive cerebral clot had required a month's stay in Albemarle Hospital, Henry died. Angelina buried him near Rosa, then sold everything he had owned, including the house on Speed Street. Within a few months, Henry's widow left Elizabeth City behind her and moved back to New York.

Leola Morgan leans back in her chair. Priscilla looks weary, her eyes shut against the late-afternoon sun.

Francis is entertaining some of the younger folks with his banter about the old days. By next Sunday, Priscilla's sister-in-law Bernice Bias Brandon will be down in Duck.

"She owns the house next door," Leola says, "but she rents it out some weeks during the summer."

Maybe Henry was born too early or died too soon. Until the civil-rights movement, no plan like his could turn out exactly the way it was envisioned. Leola Morgan explains it this way: "White people used to call down here *their* haven. I won't say *heaven*, but that's what they were probably thinking. They didn't want anyone of color coming to disturb this place. This is where they relaxed. It was fine for Negroes to come down here to work, but not fine for them to come here like they were vacationers. I think the message Henry got was, 'Don't come any closer, and don't own any of this land.'"

I wish Henry could see Priscilla's three great-grand-daughters laughing and playing on the second-level deck or spend a Sunday afternoon lounging in the living room with the members of his friend John's family. I hope he realizes that the Biases live year-round on the ocean-front in Duck. After all these years, he would be proud to know that there is a black community in the village. It may be smaller than he would have liked, but it's strong and firmly planted, hearty and thriving as sea elder.

I like to think of Henry as the guardian of Bias Shores. I like believing he knew what would eventually happen to his dream for Duck. His didn't dry up like a raisin in the sun. The truth is that dreams made on this sand may get buried, but in time, the wind brings everything to the surface, exposing the past, uncovering the sharp point of a lesson that took too long to learn.

V

Lessons of a Duck Hunter

Never kill what you won't eat. It is this tenet Frank Scarborough vividly remembers committing to memory. An adage about hunting learned the hard way, these simple words would cling like the clammy, thigh-high rubber boots he used for wading through the Currituck Sound almost fifty years before. There were certain fundamentals Frank's father, Arthur "Skip" Scarborough, was determined to impress upon his son, the sort of outdoor ethics that a youngster with a gun in a place like Duck needed to understand early.

"I was just a little guy," Frank says. "And I had this

little .22 rifle. My father had already told me over and over about not hunting anything I wouldn't eat. Well, one day, I went out with the rifle, started walking up the beach from where we lived. About half a mile north of the Caffey's Inlet Coast Guard Station, there was this old wreck sticking up a few feet above the water. A bunch of sea gulls were sitting out there on that wreck, and I was up there just wandering along when I saw them all out there. Then I got the idea. I laid down in the dunes, took my little .22 rifle, and started shooting. I don't know how he found out. Guess somebody must have told my dad I was up there hunting sea gulls.

"Well, he came out there, got me, got my rifle, got one of those sea gulls that had washed up on the beach. Then we went back to the house. He made me clean that gull first. Then he put it in a pot. He cooked that thing, just boiled it whole. And I had to eat it. It smelled like rotten fish—tasted like it, too. It was the worst thing I ever put in my mouth. I wouldn't eat another sea gull, wouldn't shoot another one again either. Never kill anything you won't eat. It was my father's hunting philosophy, and it was a good one. Still is."

Like the sea gull story, most of Frank's recollections about his boyhood in Duck come fitted with certain props—a rifle or a wooden skiff, a shovin' pole or a cargo of hand-me-down decoys, a hunting blind crowded with gun-toting kin and companions. Into each remembrance, Frank mixes good humor and an abiding affection for the characters who populated his past. His tales of being a duck hunter in Duck are as immediate and effervescent as the voice he uses to tell them. A lyrical narrator, Frank almost croons a story, his speech a rapid, rambling staccato or a slow, soothing lullaby. Every new sentence can bring a surprise, a shift in pace or tone or diction. Something unexpected is always tickling the back of Frank's throat. Spreading and shrinking like the shadows around him, his voice might echo from the base of his gut or rise in a squeak through the top of his head.

As a child, Frank digested more than the moral that came with a single rank-tasting seabird. Every boyhood experience in Duck helped shape his later life. He took in everything, swallowed whole an entire curriculum about wildlife and waterfowl and a lifestyle that could be taught only by those with enough mastery to merit the title of hunter.

Always the youngest, always considered the greenhorn, Frank met most of his idols by the time he was ten. Rough talking and hearty, these gunmen toughened their skin on northeast winds and winter dawns, on marsh islands glazed in frost or brush blinds set deep in ice-slick waters. They strengthened themselves with slow-simmering stew, toasted one another with its pungent broth, filled their bellies with its dumplings and the flesh of untamed things—the breasts of birds, the bellies of squirrels, the wings of geese, and the smooth,

MOST OF FRANK SCARBOROUGH'S BOYHOOD RECOLLECTIONS COME FITTED WITH CERTAIN PROPS—A RIFLE OR A WOODEN SKIFF, A SHOVIN' POLE OR A CARGO OF HAND-ME-DOWN DECOYS, A HUNTING BLIND CROWDED WITH GUN-TOTING KIN AND COMPANIONS. HE'S SHOWN HERE, POSING WITH THE DAY'S CATCH.

Courtesy of Frank and Sue Scarborough

firm bodies of skinned rabbits, all steeped in the same heavy pot.

Frank's heroes could be sober marksmen one day and pranksters the next. Their aim was sure and steady enough to gun down even the highest-flying waterfowl with a single bullet, their tricks so wily they could humble even the most cocksure game warden. On the undeveloped banks of the Currituck, a boy with a Remington and a pocketful of shells could grow wise and sure with these men. The early instruction Frank gleaned from them would prove as vital as the formal training he later received during a six-year enlistment in the Marine Corps and a thirty-year career in law enforcement.

Most of Frank's revered mentors are dead now. But the Tillet brothers (Avery, Al, and Clay), Jim Quidley, Walter Perry, Jay Bender, and Harry Hamilton—the locals Frank hunted beside as a boy—almost take breath and speak for themselves whenever he summons their names. Frank's childhood buddies were already adults, some of them models, others teachers and guides, all of them the only playmates he ever knew while he lived in Duck. His father's contemporaries, many of whom worked as keepers or crewmen, met and befriended Frank while the Scarborough family was stationed at Caffey's Inlet, just a few miles north of the village.

"My father's Scarborough family is actually from the Eastern Shore of Virginia," Frank says. "My father was born in Chincoteague. His father was from Maryland, a sea captain. My dad was a chief warrant officer in the Coast Guard in charge of the land-line communications for this district. That's how I got to know this area. We lived in several places, mostly Virginia Beach, but we lived down here year-round for a little while after the war, in the late '40s, when the Caffey's station was still in active service. After that, we'd come down here a lot, mostly to duck hunt.

"There were several houses around what is now the Sanderling Inn, where the people stationed at Caffey's lived. We had one of those houses, no in-door plumbing, no electricity, an outhouse in the back. It was really just a shack. My folks rented it. It never belonged to us, belonged to a guy named Harry Hamilton. Harry Hamilton was my childhood hero. Heck, he might still be my hero. He was the only man I ever knew who could shoot a green-winged teal on the wing with a .22 rifle. I mean, after all these years of hunting, I still have trouble hitting one with a damn shotgun, and this guy could do it with a .22 rifle. He might have been the greatest man I ever knew."

Today, Frank and his wife, Sue, are savoring the fruits of a long partnership and equally long professions. Their two daughters are settled and approaching middle age. Frank and Sue appreciate visits with their grand-children, the pensions that come after decades of pub-lic service, and the duck hunting they occasionally do together. Wed in the early 1960s, Frank and Sue both worked for the city of Virginia Beach. Frank retired from the police department as a lieutenant, Sue from Cook Elementary School as a language-arts teacher. They built their Duck house in 1988. When they relocated in 1991, they joined a growing number of newly retired couples living in the village year-round.

Rising above the neighboring ridge of sand hills, the Scarborough home sits back off an unpaved road in Sound Sea Village. By late morning, sun spills into every room. The floors are marbled with light, the ceilings brushed with a tincture of silver and white. There

FRANK AND SUE SCARBOROUGH PHOTOGRAPHED ON THE DECK OF THEIR HOME IN SOUTHERN SHORES.
Courtesy of Peter J. Mercier, III

are windows everywhere, and each pane seems to invite some portion of the outdoors to come in for a visit. In plain view is a pageant of filmy clouds and foaming whitecaps. Patches of winter sky float over tufts of rusty broomstraw. To the east, the Atlantic rolls and crests; to the west, the Currituck dozes flat and glossy.

"My father," Sue says laughingly, "always said, 'Only the fool builds his house on a mound of sand.'"

The Scarborough home's decor evinces meticulous care, a fondness for the nautical, a delight in things local and familial. Mementoes are spaced and hung with precision, keepsakes displayed like treasures. Ferns nest in corners; the new, tender fronds pitch and dip on the waves of a generous breeze. Some of the hunting and ornamental decoys Frank has carved himself; others he's inherited over the years. A few real ducks—long ago killed, then stuffed fat and full or mounted flat with wings spread in flight—rest over doorframes or guard archways. An artist's rendering of the Outer Banks shares wall space with a few old maps. The black smoke bomb Frank uncovered one day while surveying his sandy yard hangs between a hunk of driftwood and an old rifle. The couple's prized models of schooners and grand sailing vessels are anchored inside sparkling glass cases. A collage of family photos includes black-and-white pictures of Frank as a boy, dressed in a half-smile and a hunting jacket, crouched in front of a wood-shingled shack, rubber boots planted firmly in the sand beneath him, a half-dozen freshly shot ducks tied to a string and hanging from a raised hand.

"In the '40s," Frank says, "this area around where the house is now was still a bombing range, part of 'Navy Duck.' But I hunted right out there"—he points straight ahead, across Duck Road to the Currituck Sound—"on Caffey's Inlet Bay, in the part of the sound that's created by all those little islands."

A ship's clock clangs out the quarter-hour. Frank sits down with his last cup of morning coffee. He is outfitted like a hunter—heavy plaid flannel jacket, denim pants, boots, ball cap—but it's his forefathers' ocean-faring heritage that characterizes his face. Frank could be a storybook sea captain, his features long and angular, his complexion a healthy russet, his eyes deep set, his gaze sharp as crystal. At least a fortnight's worth of whiskers covers his cheeks and chin.

"Learned to drive along this beach behind us, a '47 Chevrolet pick-em-up truck," Frank says. "My dad used to travel up and down this part of the North Carolina coast, going to all the different stations around here, and I'd go with him. The Coast Guard had a telephone-pole line that ran right behind these dunes. Called it the Coast Guard Pole Line. There was a road—just two long ruts in the sand—that ran along there. They needed some sort of road so they could check the lines that linked all the stations. That was my dad's job. He had to make sure that communications between all these stations was maintained.

"I would get in the truck with him, and we'd start down the beach. We'd go along that road with him standing in the back of the truck and me behind the wheel. Those old vehicles had a throttle and a choke. Well, he'd have to pull the throttle out, 'cause I was too short to reach the pedals. He'd put the thing in second gear, and I'd steer. I'm seven or eight years old, sitting on a box so I'm high enough to see out the windshield, and I'm steering while he's standing up in the back of the truck checking all the wires. When he would bang on the roof, that would be my signal to stop. I'd push the throttle in, and the truck would stall. We'd ride all the way down and back on the Pole Road that way, stopping and starting.

"A lot of times, we'd have to stop because of the eagles. There were lots of them down here then, and the locals set traps for them. People around this area were still raising animals, mostly sheep and pigs. Well, they set traps for those eagles, 'cause they didn't want them carrying off their little pigs and sheep. We'd find an eagle with a steel trap on his leg, all tangled in the wire, 'cause he'd landed there and then couldn't get off. Eagles were bad for the wires. They'd mince things."

Frank and his family lived in a rented shack at Caffey's Inlet for eighteen months. As a first-grader, Frank took his share of long rides down bumpy roads. There was the thirty-five-mile round trip he made every weekday to get to school. "We rode in an old army surplus vehicle all the way from the Coast Guard station to the village of Kitty Hawk," he says. "School's not there anymore. It was real small, had all twelve grades. Maybe there were twenty of us kids altogether."

When Frank wasn't in school or balanced on a box behind the wheel of a '47 Chevy truck, he was exploring the waters around the Caffey's Inlet station in a skiff, looking for his own special hunting place or fashioning a makeshift blind out of brush. Sometimes, he'd go into the woods or the marsh to trap, but he spent most of his free time either shooting or cleaning ducks.

"There was this little island in the Currituck called Horse Island, and I had a blind out there when I was a kid. I had a ten-foot-long skiff. It was my skiff. A guy named Clay Tillet from Kitty Hawk—he was a boat maker, a decoy maker; he was in the Coast Guard—built it, and I used it. I had so many decoys in that skiff, it almost would sink. I had whatever decoys the older guys didn't want to use—nine big old canvas swan decoys, six or eight canvas goose decoys, a couple dozen duck decoys. I'm maybe nine, and I'd have that load of little decoys, and I'd push-pull my skiff out to that island. I'd hunt by myself when the older guys thought I was being a nuisance. I guess I wouldn't always sit still, or I wouldn't do this or I wouldn't do that, so they'd say, 'Go hunt by yourself,' and I'd go off.

"I'd go shoving out to Horse Island, or I'd go down

shore a little bit more to a bigger island called Waterbush Island and tie out my decoys. I'd build little blinds, maybe just some bushes I'd stick down there in the mud and hide behind. I'd only be out there a little while, and I'd kill my limit. Then I'd be back at the house having breakfast, and they'd all come back in around ten or eleven, and they hadn't killed nothing. I'd have all I was allowed to have, maybe even some more, and they hadn't even seen anything.

"Course, sometimes, I might go someplace I wasn't supposed to—rest areas around the gun clubs, places that were off limits or where you weren't supposed to shoot. I might sneak in there. Of course, if I'd been caught, I'd of been in real big trouble. But I might have done it anyway." Frank laughs. "As a little kid, I wasn't always on the up and up. I usually had to learn my lessons the hard way. That may explain why I spent so much time hunting on my own."

Nature and isolation were steadfast companions for a boy who lived on the North Banks a half-century ago. Without electricity, decent roads, or the opportunity to socialize with pals his own age, Frank shadowed men almost twice his size or traveled alone in a skiff on the sound. Today, he describes those months of solitary childhood as if they were a gift.

"Duck wasn't much back then," he says. "It's probably hard for anyone who didn't see it until now to imagine what is was like. Going into the main part of the village from here, there were a few houses. Some of them are still there. And that building that's Bob's Tackle Shop, it used to be a store—maybe Ned Rodgers owned it. I used to trap muskrats up here, load 'em up in my skiff, and trade 'em for shotgun shells at that store. I'd push-pull my way down the sound with a shovin' pole. It would take just about all day to get there and back. There were no restaurants and just that one store, but my daddy loved to hunt, and I grew up eating all kinds of ducks, all kinds of fish. That was our staple diet, one or the other.

"There weren't any kids to play with. Maybe once or twice, one would come up here. It was only three miles from the center of the village to the station, but it might have been a hundred. I grew up in an adult world. It was always adults who were around. It was all I knew. Duck didn't have much, but it was a great place to grow up."

After his family moved back across the Virginia line, Frank still hunted the Currituck Banks with his dad and older brother.

By the late 1940s, many turn-of-the-century gun clubs built by Northern investors on the Outer Banks were still in operation, though most had already reached their zeniths. During the early decades of the twentieth century, a small number of visiting duck hunters frequented the Powder Ridge, Duck's first and only gun club, a simple A-frame house made handsome by cedar shingles and a fine screened porch for watching sunsets over the sound. Two six-foot whalebones, ribs blanched as sand, formed a decorative **X** high over the front entrance.

Like larger clubs farther north along the Currituck, the Powder Ridge was owned by absentee investors—some say they were brokers from Wall Street—and managed by a local, Lewis Scarborough, a village native who lived there with his wife and family during the 1930s. Ann Susan, a black woman who traveled across the Currituck from her home on the mainland, spent a few cold months every year living in a little house tucked into the pines near the club.

A few village locals still remember Susan. They claim she was the first black person they ever met in Duck. She won the hearts of visitors and residents alike. Her cooking tempted the village boys to take a detour to the Powder Ridge on their way to school. They hoped there would be some scraps left over from the hearty hunter breakfasts she prepared before sunup. And Susan rarely failed them, always making enough to round out the stomachs of hunters and schoolboys on a cold Duck morning.

By the 1930s, recreational duck hunting was already beginning to wane. Some blame the Great Depression for paring the number of would-be gunmen and making winter vacations shooting waterfowl on the North Banks no longer easily affordable. More likely, though, it was the federal government's legislation that dulled interest in the sport. Each year brought more stringent guidelines about season lengths and bag limits, about the types of guns and decoys hunters could use, about the style and location of the blinds they could build.

But the steadily growing weight of government regulations couldn't sink the enthusiasm of one boy who was already an ardent duck hunter. "Another benefit I had through my father was getting a chance to hunt the gun clubs around here," Frank says. "During World War II, he talked the Coast Guard into putting telephones in any of the hunt clubs that still had somebody left at them, usually a maintenance person or a caretaker. The reason for that was it increased the number of people to watch the coast. Down here, you had the Whalehead, Currituck Beach, and Pine Island Gun Clubs. My father put telephones in each one of them, and in turn, for having free contact with the outside world, they would report any unusual comings and goings, any happenings or emergencies. It enlarged the Coast Guard's span of communication.

"As a result of my father's getting them this telephone service, the gun clubs allowed him to hunt, and I would go with him. We hunted all these gun clubs. The Currituck Club was and still is exactly the same as the way it was in 1850. It's probably the oldest continuous hunt club in the South, maybe the oldest on the entire East Coast of the United States. Whalehead, they're trying to restore it right now. After I was grown, my brother and I and some other guys rented that place, paid a thousand dollars a year to use it. We hunted there for five or six years. The Pine Island Club was the one closest to where I had lived at Caffey's Inlet, and we hunted there when I was a kid. They had probably ten bedrooms, maybe twenty hunters, two to a room, staying there at the same time. They were what we called 'gentlemen hunters,' mostly from the North, guys who had a lot of money to spend. They were either friends of the owners that were invited in as guests or actual members of the gun club. See, back then, you had to have some connections, either be a friend of a club owner or an actual member of a club, or you didn't hunt there. Except for men like my dad, anyone who had done the clubs a favor, then they'd give you a place when the club wasn't full.

"Every club had its own rules about hunting. For instance, at Pine Island, you didn't go out before sunup. Carl White owned the place, and he had this philosophy that if you went out there before dawn and you scared the ducks off, they wouldn't come back. There was some merit to that way of thinking. A lot of the time, it was true, and it would happen. They eventually passed a law that you couldn't even leave the landing until a half-hour before sunrise.

"Most times at Pine Island, hunters would get up about 5 A.M., have breakfast, and then go out and shoot

Frank Scarborough and his dad, Arthur "Skip" Scarborough, posing with Frank's catch in front of the Caffey's Inlet Coast Guard Station, where they lived in the 1940s.
Courtesy of Frank and Sue Scarborough

till 10 or 11, depending on how long it took them to get to their limit. Limits would vary from year to year, but the maximum was usually around twelve ducks per hunter per day. I can remember when I was kid, I'd be looking in the old logbooks, seeing entries from the days when hunters still used sink boxes and iron decoys. I liked reading some of those entries: 'Went out at 8 o'clock, set the sink box, hunted for four hours. Wasn't a very good day, only killed six hundred canvasback.'"

Frank laughs. "Imagine that. It's not a very good day, and he's killed six hundred canvasback."

Record waterfowl kills are the stuff of North Banks legend. On what would eventually become known as a golden day of hunting in 1905, brothers Russell and Van Griggs spent all morning and afternoon shooting into the air over the Currituck. In less than ten hours, they killed 892 ruddy ducks. The story includes details about Russell's gun. It got so hot, some say, he had to keep dipping it into the sound between rounds to cool it off.

Feats like the Griggses' occurred only prior to the government's strict bag limits. Before game wardens waited at the landing to count the dead birds heaped in the bottoms of boats, North Banks gunmen might make a few swaggering wagers, openly contending for the honor of shooting the greatest number of ducks and geese in a single day. At the close of the nineteenth century, filling barrels with dead waterfowl was a matter of local economic survival. In the years between the Civil War and the Migratory Bird Treaty Act of 1918, commercial hunting flourished on the North Banks.

Back then, when the skies over the sound might fill with as many as ten thousand Canada geese flocking from every direction, hunters hid in sink boxes—what the old-timers called "batteries," wooden containers shaped like coffins with rigid decking, maybe three feet wide, attached to each side. Every exposed surface of a sink box was finished with coats of slate gray, making it virtually undetectable to ducks and other hunters. Four free-floating wings gave the battery some buoyancy, allowing it to rise and fall according to the movement of the water. Anchors helped secure the box in place, a heavy one stationed at the head, a lighter one dragging like a tail. Hunters used other moveable ballast—a covey of iron birds, each weighing at least twenty-five pounds—for sinking their boxes. Every weight was tied to one of the slicks, the wooden decoys that floated around the battery. In still waters, a hunter might position 10 or 12 of these metal decoys around the edge of his box. If conditions changed, he could drop a few of the decoys off, thereby lifting the battery just enough to keep water from pouring in over the sides. Painted to match the 150 or more wooden slicks each hunter set out in the sound, the metal decoys seemed as much lures as protection for the hidden gunmen.

Batteries afforded just enough room for a single hunter to lie flat on his back, his head propped on a cushion or pillow, his eyes barely level with the rim of the box. Automatics and repeaters were luxuries reserved for a future generation of sport hunters. Most of these professional gunmen used two breechloaders, both ten-gauge, both double-barreled with hammers. The ends of their thirty-two-inch muzzles balanced against the footboards of their sink boxes, they'd watch and wait. By sunrise, birds would fall out of the skies in a shower as heavy as hail. Hunters readied their weapons, aimed, and fired, hundreds of shots piercing the morning stillness and the flesh of unsuspecting prey.

In the early 1880s, Herbert H. Brimley, a zoologist who visited the North Banks to collect specimens of local waterfowl for the North Carolina State Museum in Raleigh, recorded his observations of nineteenth-century market hunters at work on the Currituck. "At its best," he wrote, "a battery was always a clumsy affair and awkward to handle, and setting one out and taking it up again on a cold, windy day was no job for weaklings. . . . I have tried this method of shooting on a number of occasions but have nearly always had better luck shooting from a blind, though the battery was a deadly method of taking waterfowl when practiced by experienced professionals. . . . On the Currituck, bags of a hundred a day from a battery were not rare enough to get one's name in the paper."

After icing was introduced in 1874, hunters could preserve ducks for shipping up north, a practice that continued until the government banned the sale of migratory waterfowl. As a child, Ruth Scarborough Tate used to stencil company names on wooden barrels before her brothers and father packed them with layers of ice and the carcasses of redheads and canvasbacks or ruddy ducks and buffleheads. Hundreds of chilled ducks would be loaded on freight boats for Elizabeth City or Norfolk, then transported by rail to urban destinations farther west and north.

Cash on the spot from regular buyers meant some local commercial hunters might earn as much as a hundred dollars a day during the winter months. Individual incomes varied, the profits dependent upon the size of the hunter's kill and the species of duck he gunned down. Back then, waterfowl were typically sold in pairs. Canvasbacks and redheads brought the best price, their market value ranging anywhere from one to four dollars for each twosome. The average cost for smaller ducks—ruddies, teals, and buffleheads—was fifty cents a pair, but even these less meaty birds could merit double that amount if out-of-town buyers were hungry enough to pay it. By comparison, Canada geese seemed a bargain, never more expensive than fifty cents and generally plentiful enough to be sold at half price.

Duck's market hunters weren't the only ones to

benefit financially from the waterfowl that flocked to the Currituck. Industrious young villagers began to appreciate the weak shots—those gunmen who left behind "cripples," ducks that were wounded but not dead. Early risers combed through the marsh grass bordering the sound, searching out the injured birds and capturing them to be killed. "If a boy got up before daylight," Ruth Scarborough Tate recalls, "he could make twenty-five dollars in a morning."

By the 1920s, the federal ban on the sale of migratory waterfowl was in effect, and most commercial hunters in Duck turned to fishing as their primary means of support. Fortunately, North Banks gun clubs were attracting recreational hunters to the banks of the Currituck. Visiting sportsmen no longer needed to wait for the "bluebird" days when the market hunters didn't bother to go out. Gun clubs couldn't rival what the locals had netted from commercial hunting, but they did offer a few Duck natives other job opportunities. To provide their guests with guides, gun-club owners might hire the same men who had been forced to relinquish their own lucrative hunting careers a few years before.

"There was this guy from Duck," Frank says. "His name was Shepard Perry. He's dead now, but he was a guide and a guard at Pine Island when I was hunting there with my dad. They had two guard shacks, one at either end of the club, and Perry lived in one of those shacks year-round. He would watch for trespassers or check out conditions on the marsh and get the blinds ready. He'd work as a guard all the time and as a guide during the hunting season."

Frank has seen a few batteries, but he's never hunted in one. By the time he was old enough to aim a gun at a bird on the North Banks, those old-fashioned sink boxes, like the heyday of commercial waterfowl hunting, were gone.

"They outlawed sink boxes, I guess, sometime before the '40s," he says. "They weren't fair to the ducks. You could set them out in the middle of the sound, and the ducks couldn't see the hunters. It just gives the hunters too much of an opportunity. There's a similar type of blind today, called a float bind. It's legal, a blind that floats, but I think it has to have at least eighteen or twenty inches sticking up above the water.

"Now, mostly, they use two kinds of blinds, a marsh blind built on the land and a deepwater or bush blind, one that's actually built out on the water to simulate a little island. All blinds are basically still boxes. A deepwater blind is made out of plywood, about four feet wide and anywhere from eight to twelve feet long, depending on how many men you want to fit in there, and it's up on poles probably three or four feet above the water. The back is usually eight feet high; maybe you put a little cover on it so you don't get rain running down your neck. You usually build a bench seat

across the back for the hunters to sit on, and there's a door at one end so you can get in and out of it. The front is only about four feet high. You can see over it even when you're sitting down. You get pine and bushes, and you cover it all up. You bring your boat around to the back of the blind, anchor it, and then make your hide, sticking more brush down into the water so the ducks won't see the boat moving and get scared away. It all ends up looking like a little island."

Unlike battery boxes, where hunters lay flat for hours and worried about keeping the water from washing over the sides, contemporary blinds make waiting out a cold morning and the hunt for ducks a little more comfortable.

"Some blinds can be pretty fancy," Frank says. "I've seen blinds that had little rooms built on the back with cots in them. We used to keep a stove in our blinds. Yeah, we'd cook up some soup on a little one-burner that we'd set up."

"Those were the days," Sue says, "when the only thing that might chase the ducks away was the smell of kerosene."

Frank chuckles at a memory just beginning to take shape. "I remember one time, right out here on an island called Wallow Marsh, my daddy had this blind with another fellow, a guy named Clay Tillet, a legend in my mind. Well, we were all out there, Clay, my brother, my daddy, and me. I was about ten, and I had on those rubber boots that go all the way to your crotch. It was real cold, and my feet were freezing. I mean I was just about crying, they were so cold. Clay lit the stove so he could get some soup going. So I got over to where I could put my feet under the stove. It was real quiet, everybody just looking around for ducks. Then I hear my brother start sniffing. 'You smell something?' my brother says. 'What is that smell?' 'I don't know,' my dad says. 'Stinks like something's burning.' Well, I looked down, and sure enough, my boots were on fire! I set my boots on fire. Feet weren't cold anymore after that."

Nothing, not even a few childhood blunders and scares, ever discouraged Frank from hunting.

"Another time, it was in November, on a really bad day. The wind was blowing particularly hard, and it was awfully cold. I had to take this man, Dr. Allen—he was a heart doctor—out to hunt. He wasn't a very good hunter, just visiting down here and wanted to do it. Somebody at Caffey's probably owed him a favor or something. I was maybe eleven or twelve years old, and I would end up having to take a lot of these visiting guys out hunting because the older guys, my dad and the others, they couldn't be bothered. But somebody had to go out with these guys, 'cause they didn't know what they were doing. So I'd push-pull them out to the blind, tie out the decoys, fix the blind if it needed it, pick up the ducks if they shot any, that sort of thing. 'Let Frank do it,' that's what they'd say.

"Well, at that time, we were still hunting out of Caffey's Inlet, on a bush blind that stuck up out of the water, what they called the Station Slough Blind, because that was the one blind the guys stationed at Caffey's could use whenever they wanted. Other people hunted there, but it was really for the men at Caffey's, one of these unwritten things that everybody knew. Well, they said, 'You take Dr. Allen out to the Station Slough Blind,' and I said okay.

"We get in the boat, and I shoved us on out there. It was a bad day, real cold and windy, so it took us a pretty long time. I got Dr. Allen in the blind, and then I started putting out the decoys, maybe sixty or seventy of 'em. These damned decoys kept turning over 'cause there was ice on them. I'd already gone out a couple of times to knock the ice off of 'em.

"We were out there a little while when I noticed that the water around us was starting to freeze up. We'd shot some ducks, and I saw that the ice was starting to move. The wind was coming from the north, and the water was freezing up and moving along. I realized that the ice had moved down on that blind and crushed the sides of the boat hide. I couldn't get the boat out. That blind was in a slough, in the deeper part of the water. I told the doctor, 'It's bad. We gotta get out of here, and the only way we can get out of here is to walk.' We had to get overboard, and so I told him, 'It's only about five hundred yards from here to the landing. If we keep moving, we'll be wet, but we'll be all right, 'cause we won't be far from the house.'

"We grabbed our guns and got in the water. It was about chest deep on me. The water wasn't that cold once you got used to it, but what I didn't realize was that the same ice that crushed the blind was all around us. Everything was freezing up. I had to break the ice with my elbows so I could walk us through the water. Well, we didn't go twenty yards before Dr. Allen had a heart attack. He was in bad shape. I could tell something was really wrong, and I was only a kid. He must of known he was having a heart attack. I got him back to the blind and put him in the boat, and then I knew I had to get to the landing.

"I'm breaking the ice with my elbows, trying to get to the station so I can get help. It seemed like it took a long time going through the water that way. Well, I eventually got to the landing, then to the station. My dad and the others figured we were in trouble. Other hunters had been out that morning on other blinds, and they couldn't get their boats back through that ice either. My dad and the others, they went back out to the blind in a surfboat. They took Dr. Allen to the station, and I think they got a Coast Guard helicopter to take him to a hospital on the mainland. Lucky for me, he didn't die. It was pretty scary for a kid."

After he and Sue married, Frank was a full-time police officer and a part-time college student. But during the winters, he moonlighted at several nearby gun clubs in Virginia Beach as a hunting guide, a job for which he'd already rigorously trained. "Those trips I took with guys like Dr. Allen, they really were my first guide jobs, though I didn't realize it then.

"For the first twenty years of my life, I never realized the importance of having a good hunting dog either," Frank says. "We never had dogs early on. I guess we thought that bringing a dog along would just be a nuisance."

Sue laughs. "The men he used to hunt with, they

would say that Frank was their hunting dog," she says. "He was always the youngest, so that was his job, to go collect all the dead ducks."

"Whenever a bunch of us would go out hunting, I'd have to go out and pick up the ducks that had been shot. A lot of times, I was the only one who could find 'em," Frank says. "It was like I had a sixth sense or something. If a duck is shot down in the marsh, even if it's dead, it's really hard to find because of the color. Take a female mallard, for instance. They're very dull, about the same color as grass. I could find 'em when nobody else could. It was like I could almost smell 'em. I had a good eye where they went.

"When I was a kid, I had this big hunting coat, and it had these deep pockets inside. I would just pick up all the ducks I found on the marsh and stick 'em into those pockets. Then I'd walk back to the boat, take 'em out, and lay 'em over the seat so that their heads hung down toward the bottom of the boat. That way, if the duck was bleeding, it could all drain out. I always carried some string with me, and after a while, I'd tie all the ducks by their feet to long pieces of string and then sling 'em over my shoulder and carry 'em all up to the house from the landing that way.

"When I was a real little kid living down here, we used to take my ducks and hang 'em on an outside wall of the house. Older people around here had this thing about ducks. They'd let 'em hang for two or three days to get the gaminess—that wild taste—out of 'em before they'd eat 'em. I knew people who'd hang ducks by the head, and they wouldn't even bother to clean 'em until the duck's head had rotted off and the body fell on the ground. But when I shot a duck, I'd take it back up to the house and almost start cleaning it right away.

"It's work cleaning a duck. Ducks have fur on 'em as well as feathers. You'd have to get all the wing feathers off first. Then you'd fill a big pan with alcohol and light it. You'd have to hold the duck above the flame and turn it until you singed all the rest of the down and feathers off. Some people would just skin 'em. Some people would just take the breast out and throw the rest of it away. But for me, it depends on what kind of duck I have. A marsh duck—a mallard, gadwall, wigeon, pintail—I usually pick 'em, take the insides out, and keep the whole duck, skin and all. A diving duck—like a blackhead or a lesser or greater scaup—I usually pick 'em or skin 'em. Then there's the blue Peters, what we call coots. You just skin 'em, 'cause all you have is the breast and legs anyhow. They're just a little duck. Some people won't even bother to shoot a coot, but I love 'em. They're a great-tasting duck."

Dead blue Peters may have been the only type of waterfowl federal game wardens never worried about counting too carefully. In the 1940s and 1950s, when the limit on most species ranged from six to twelve, a

North Banks hunter could still shoot as many as twenty coots a day.

Fifty years ago, game wardens still haunted the North Banks. By most accounts, the locals thought of them as favorably as they did a northeaster on Christmas or a hurricane on the Fourth of July. Duck hunters had felt indignant about the wardens' arrival three decades earlier, when they first started waiting at the landings, tallying and admonishing, reciting regulations like scripture.

Enjoying the power that came with an official badge, some wardens just seemed to take their jobs too seriously. They certified their authority with fancy documents, twisted their tongues around the language of a mainland bureaucracy most Bankers never wanted to understand. After 1918, commercial hunting of migratory waterfowl might lead to an arrest and a felony conviction. Exceeding bag limits usually meant the threat of a heavy fine. But for any hunter who was a surfman or a keeper at one of the North Banks Coast Guard stations, there were other risks as well.

"My father was very cognizant about limits and game regulations because of the position he had," Frank says. "If someone was convicted of a game violation, then the Coast Guard would say, 'You're out of here. You've been convicted of a felony. Your career is over.' It could affect a man's future. It wasn't just the job they'd lose, it was losing the retirement, too. Yeah, a game violation could be pretty serious, especially if it was market hunting, if a hunter was selling ducks.

"Those game wardens were always coming around. They had one warden down here that was particularly disliked. I think his name was Ross. He might of been somebody's kin, married to somebody's daughter.

"One guy we hunted with, Jim Quidley, he had a boat we called the Red Eye. Why we called it that, I never knew. He kept a deepwater blind down a ways, where the Barrier Island Station Restaurant is today. Jim was a good hunter, but he was a really good carver. He had carved this decoy of a dead duck. I mean, this thing was made of wood, but it looked so good you couldn't tell the difference.

"Well, this game warden Ross, he was unrelenting, wouldn't give an inch, wouldn't budge even a little. So Jim says, 'I'll tell you what. I'll get that son of a bitch. You wait and see.'

"One day, Jim's out there hunting in his blind, and he sees that game warden, ol' Ross, up at the landing. The limit was five, and Jim comes in with six dead ducks in the bottom of his boat. Ol' Ross, he sees Jim and starts counting. 'I got you now,' Ross says to Jim. 'I got you now. You got six ducks, and you're only supposed to have five. I've got you now.'

"So Jim says, 'Well, asshole, you got me then. You got me, and I guess you better just take me to jail. That's what you better do.'

"Well, Ross is smiling, 'cause he's thinking he's got something on somebody, and Jim, he's smiling, too. Ross starts going for those ducks. He's grabbing 'em up. Then, all of a sudden, he reaches in and realizes something's not right. One of them dead ducks was the decoy Jim had made out of wood and stuck down in that boat. Ol' Ross, he was so embarrassed, he didn't come around for two weeks."

By the mid-1950s, North Banks land was becoming less and less accessible to area sportsmen. The liberty that duck hunters had previously known in choosing sites for blind building faded like the stenciling on decades-old barrels once filled with freshly shot waterfowl pressed between layers of ice. Electricity and a few improved roads heralded a modern village, and a change of attitude seemed to accompany the private ownership of even an acre or two of Duck property. Every marshy island no bigger than a freckle dotting the face of the Currituck would eventually belong to someone. By then, the Coast Guard had shut down operations at Caffey's Inlet, and a man named Carl Wright held a deed for the land on which the shacks and station house stood. It was Carl who decided the time had come for Frank's old hunting buddies to move on.

"Carl got . . . Well, let's say he got sort of . . ."

Sue tries finishing Frank's thought. "Uncooperative," she says.

"Well, maybe, but he got sort of uppity, and he booted everybody out. He made them actually move their blinds off the islands out there by the station. So they moved down this way, to this next street right over here." Frank motions with his head to the south. "That's how come I have this property, 'cause of this fellow named Walter Perry.

"Walter was one the contemporaries we hunted with. When he heard about Carl's kicking us off his land, Walter said, 'Well, fellas, I know. I got some property down here. We'll just all move down to my land.'

"So we moved our hunting locations down here. Walter built this little place on the sound, right across the street from here, called the Boar's Nest. It was nothing but a land house, but we called it that because that's where he stayed. His wife always lived in the brick house they owned in Kitty Hawk, and he lived down here in the Boar's Nest almost all year round.

"I was still pretty young when Carl Wright kicked everybody off his land, and they all moved down here to Walter's. We were already living in Virginia Beach, but I was always hanging around in Duck hunting the shoreline.

"Walter, now, he loved to cook. That was his big thing. Everybody would go out hunting at daylight, but Walter would come back to the Boar's Nest around ten and start cooking—ducks, turtles, crabs, whatever he had. When I was a kid, he would call me in. 'Here,' he'd say, and then he'd give me a pocketful of shells for the Remington .28 shotgun I had. 'Go to the beach,' he'd say. 'Kill everything you can, except those damn sea gulls. I ain't eating no damn sea gull.'

"Back then, there would be water standing all out here, like little ponds, and there'd be ducks and birds all over the place, so I'd go out and shoot robins, woodpeckers, ducks, squirrels. I'd shoot anything I could except the sea gulls, and I'd bring it all back to him. I might have killed six or eight birds and maybe a rabbit or something like that. Well, he'd take those birds and just cut the breasts out and pop them into the pot, clean the rabbit or the squirrel and throw him in there, then stew it all together until the meat fell off the bones. Just before it was done, he'd take those canned biscuits and throw them in to make dumplings. We'd eat every drop of that stew for lunch. Walter always fixed it. It was good-tasting stuff."

Frank portrays Walter Perry as having more celebrity than most of the other master duck hunters he knew. To a boy, Walter must have seemed a hero, a guardian who reclaimed a threatened tradition; his investment meant there would be other blinds to hunt on, and the Boar's Nest gave a sort of rough-hewn sanctuary to his Caffey's companions. But it was Walter's generous spirit, seasoned with a dash of the unpredictable, that makes him as savory in Frank's memory as the game stews he once concocted for himself and his fellow gunmen on winter afternoons.

Originally from the North Banks, Walter served in the Coast Guard, then worked as a homicide detective for the Washington, D.C., police department. He asserted some influence in the community, talking politics when he had to as chairman of the school board or as a county commissioner.

"When I was ten, Walter was probably forty," Frank says. "Even after I was a grown man, already been in and out of the service, I was still a kid to him. Even after I was a police officer, when I thought myself an equal, I'd be down here hunting, but I never stopped being a boy as far as those guys were concerned. I knew Walter a long time. He was a good man, a good friend."

Regardless of where Walter was working, he always came back to the Currituck to hunt, always maintained a residence somewhere in the area. After he retired, Walter moved back into the Boar's Nest; he returned to Duck to live off the same land he had bought and shared, the same land he and Frank had hunted on years before, the same land that would eventually become the subdivision where Frank and Sue built a retirement house of their own.

"Even though I had grown up here, spent lots of time down here hunting, there was nothing here for me to do after I got out of the service," Frank says. "There wasn't work that paid very much, so men had to move away to look for jobs, but most of them came back, or thought about coming back.

"When I was grown and married, we'd come down here to hunt with Walter. He had a blind out there called the Smoke House, 'cause he was always cooking out there, always cooking.

"After my daddy died, my brother and I were both living in Virginia Beach. We'd come down here and hunt on a blind called Wallow Marsh. One time, it was in the '60s, we wanted to come down here and hunt, but it was Christmas Eve day. Our wives had said, 'Okay, you can go hunting on Christmas Eve day, but make sure you're home early enough so that we can have dinner, so you can spend some time with the kids, help put their toys together after they go to bed. And *don't drink too much.*' So we said, 'No problem.'

"We come down here about five in the morning. Before we go out hunting, Walter says, 'At noontime, when you boys come back in, make sure that you stay and have Christmas dinner. I'm making my Christmas dinner early because all of you-all are here now.'

"Walter was probably already in his sixties by then, still living in the Boar's Nest, but he'd enlarged it by this time, built another room on the side and enclosed the porch along the front. The porch stretched across the house, maybe fifteen feet long, and he put a big ol' wooden table in there, like a picnic bench, but it was probably ten feet long.

"There was my brother and I, Shepard Perry—he

was damn near eighty—and two or three other fellas down here. I told Walter, 'We have got to get home early. We came down here this morning, but it's Christmas Eve, and we've got to get home as quick as we can.'

"Walter says, 'That's right. I understand. I understand, but you got to come back at noon.'

"So we came back to the Boar's Nest around noontime, and dinner wasn't ready. Walter was busy fixing moose, some turtle stew, other stuff, all of it game. Of course, the other guys who were already in there, they didn't care if dinner was late, 'cause they had already been passing the bottle around. Walter says to my brother and me, 'Boys, it's going to be ready in just a minute. You just got to stay. That's all there is to it.' Well, needless to say, we stayed. We knew we were gonna be late getting home. We knew we didn't need to eat there, but it was sort of an obligation, a hunting obligation.

"Walter had gone out and cut down a cedar tree. He had it standing in the corner, all decorated up for Christmas with whiskey bottle tops and beer cans. He may have had some lights on it. Around three o'clock, dinner's finally ready. Walter's two coon dogs—little terriers—were sleeping next to the table. So we all sit down, pass the bottle, share the grace.

"Just as we're getting ready to eat, this guy, Jay Bender—he was a wild man—comes up in his truck.

He pulls up in the yard. We could see him through the windows on the porch. Jay was a friend of Walter's, a friend of all of ours. Well, Walter says, 'Guess I better get another plate.' Then we thought we saw that there was somebody with Jay, so Walter says, 'Well, I guess I better get two more plates.'

"Jay has something in his hands. He comes up to the door, opens it just a little, and hollers, 'Hey, Walter, I know how much you like these, so looky here what I just caught for you down the road!' And with that, Jay throws something into the porch. It was a raccoon, and it wasn't very happy about having been caught, either. Well that damned raccoon starts scrambling around on the floor, and those two terriers that were laying there, well, they see that raccoon, that raccoon sees those dogs, and they all start running around the room. We're still sitting there, my brother and I, and we're trying to eat real fast so we can get home. We all gotta hold our feet up while the dogs are yapping and chasing that raccoon around in circles under the table.

"The next thing that raccoon sees is the Christmas tree in the corner. So up the tree that raccoon goes, the dogs right after him, *grrr ruff-ruff, grrr ruff-ruff, grrr ruff-ruff.* Those dogs are circling the bottom of that tree, the raccoon's up there trying to hang on, this little ol' cedar tree, it's rocking back and forth. Jay's laughing. We're all trying to eat, 'cause we want to get out of there.

"So Walter says, 'Damn you, Jay Bender. This is terrible. You're interrupting my guests' meal. I was gonna feed you and be nice to you, and you throw that raccoon in here and cause all this trouble. Now, he's up in my damned Christmas tree, and I can't get them damned dogs off him. There's only one way to solve this damn problem.'

"Walter reaches over, grabs his shotgun. *Boom.* He shoots the damn raccoon right in the house, right out of that tree. Christmas ornaments fly all over the place. Raccoon flies all over the place. The raccoon falls out of the tree. He's dead, and the dogs are yapping all over him.

"Then Walter turns around and says, 'And damn you, too, Jay Bender. You've ruined everything, and you're next.' *Boom.* He cranks off a round at Jay. It hits the wall next to the door.

"Jay's jumping and dodging the spray of bullets and saying, 'Whoo, whoo.' Then he runs outside, jumps in his truck. Walter's standing in the door, and Jay's spinning his truck around in the yard trying to get away. Walter cranks off another round, then another round. I don't think he was actually aiming at Jay, but he let another one rip over the top of Jay's truck.

"We finished eating, got home real late, probably drank more than we were supposed to, probably got in trouble for it, too, but it was an afternoon I'll never forget."

Eventually, Walter Perry did what most people who owned land in Duck did during the eighties. He divided what was to become Sound Sea Village into parcels and started selling building lots, just a few every year, to supplement his retirement.

"Walter was quite a character. He would forget what he'd sold and end up selling the same lots more than once," Sue says. "We bought this lot, and about three times after that, Walter would call us up and say, 'Hey, I sold your lot again. Would you like to swap?'"

"I bought the land this house is on from Walter for three thousand dollars," Frank says. "Now, building lots here are selling for twenty times that much."

Frank and Sue have recently purchased another lot, but this one is not in Sound Sea Village or in Duck.

"We're moving," Frank says. His voice is getting hoarse; he speaks in a low hush, almost a whisper. "Yeah, we bought a lot in Southern Shores, on the sound, and now we're in the process of getting plans together. We're gonna build a house there. It's just too rough here. It's not really a neighborhood atmosphere."

"It's lonely, it's bleak, it's cold and windy," Sue says. "This house is built more for the summer weather, but in the winter, it starts rocking."

"The loneliness doesn't bother me," Frank says. "It bothers Sue, but I was used to that from growing up down here. I guess I thought that by coming back here to Duck, there would be . . . Well, I knew it wasn't going to be exactly the same. It's changed, and I've seen that change occur over the years. But I had hoped that there would be some of it left, that I could go back to hunting here again."

"We have a place for a blind," Sue says.

"Yeah," Frank says, head lowered, fingers tapping the table. "I have a license for a location out there on the sound where I can build a blind." He strokes his bearded chin. "But I have never gotten anybody interested enough to help me. The only hunting I do now is with Sue. We go and do a lottery thing to get a blind down at the federal game preserve.

"But that's not the same thing. The guys I used to hunt with right out here, they're all gone now. Just about all of them are dead except for my brother, and he still lives in Virginia Beach."

Frank leans back and stretches. "Yup," he says, "we're leaving Duck and going to Southern Shores." Then he turns away and looks through the window, as if waiting for someone to walk out of his past and over the low, bald dunes that separate his sandy yard from the next one.

Outside, a gentle wind ruffles the cordgrass. Inside, the ship's clock clangs long and loud.

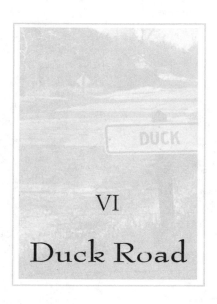

VI

Duck Road

Only one road leads to Duck, the same solitary course that runs through the heart of the village. Today, it could be a jeweler's display case, a stretch of tar and asphalt as lustrous as cut diamonds on black velvet. Just a single lane in and a single lane out, it's the sole route that guides you back.

The North Carolina Department of Transportation has maintained this northern section of N.C. 12 for almost forty years. From N.C. 158 in Kitty Hawk, it commences a twenty-five-mile path, four through Southern Shores and almost another four through Duck.

Duck Road has long been the main artery of the village. This photograph shows the village before the recent development boom.

Courtesy of the Outer Banks History Center

Then it weaves its way to Caffey's Inlet, twines past Ocean Pines and Sanderling, lopes over the Currituck County line until it reaches the Corolla Lighthouse, where, not far below the Virginia border, it dead-ends in a small mountain of sand. No matter what name the state or county gives it, no matter when or where they find themselves on it, to the locals, this section of N.C. 12 has always been Duck Road.

Duck Road has long been the main artery of the village. Running along the edge of the Currituck, where the villagers built their houses decades ago, it helped shape the neighborhood. By the 1970s, Duck Road proved itself a credible augur, foreshadowing every metamorphosis and predicting every change. Villagers recall the sight of road crews, men in yellow hard hats, the rumble of county or state trucks, the stench of oil. Their senses told them to brace for something new. Another transformation must be looming on the horizon. Every extension of Duck Road presaged one more transition for the village.

Until 1944, the Department of Transportation had no record of any road in Duck, though there had always been a rough, wet course along the Currituck, a bumpy, rutted path that took a traveler around the sound-side woods and into the village. By 1952, a graded and drained sand road ran north from the 158 cutoff in Kitty Hawk to a little less than a mile past the entrance to Duck. A year later, almost four miles of

roadway from Southern Shores northward were relocated to the east—away from the Currituck Sound—
covered with tar and stone, and given an official name,
County Road 90. Then an additional county road, this
one numbered 91, attached another half-mile of graded
roadway north of Duck.

There was still no surfaced road to Caffey's Inlet
or Sanderling until 1957, when County Road 1, four
miles of earth and sand, was graded and drained. In
1961, County Roads 90, 91, and 1 became a state road,
and officials numbered it 12. By the late 1980s, the
entire portion from Southern Shores in Dare County
to Corolla in Currituck County became part of the
larger N.C. 12. The state widened it, improved its surface, paved each mile with development in mind,
glossed every inch of it for a new season of tourists.

Once bordered by oaks and pines and a smattering
of widely spaced, simple houses, Duck Road showed
the most visible signs of transformation when the village "center," now a multimillion-dollar shopping district, began taking shape in the early 1980s. As trees
fell and backhoes scooped out the deep roots, retirees
from points north and entrepreneurs in pursuit of a
golden business opportunity laid claim to the village.
So, too, did a few real-estate developers, property man-
agers, support staff, spouses, and children. For more
than a decade, this trend continued. Voter registration
records reveal Duck's resident population to have more

than tripled, from 94 registered voters in 1980 to 291 in 1995. These same records indicate changing economics and politics, the percentage of Democrats steadily declining and that of Republicans continually rising.

But the old-timers didn't need to examine voter registration records to know what was happening to their community. They just watched Duck Road. Each time the state took it another few yards north, finally dragging it over the county line, the village seemed to shrink, acres of open space swapped for another commercial building or residential subdivision. More road or improved road, it made no difference. Either way, unfamiliar faces and unfamiliar ways found an easier entrance into Duck.

Like most of the village's original daughters, Ruth Scarborough Tate soon understood the value of being an early riser, especially in the summer. Having lived a long time without the cool luxury of air conditioning in her modest, flesh-colored house on Duck Road, she learned from experience that cooking and cleaning were forenoon work. Whatever needed to be done should be finished by lunch, before the sun baked the wooden shingles and scorched the tin or tarpaper roofs.

Every homemaker with a lick of good sense understood that morning was the only advisable time for doing daily chores. Village lore was a powerful stimulus. It cautioned wives that bad luck would befall them if they were foolish enough to sweep sand out their front doors after sundown.

In the 1930s, the high heat of a summer midday was meant for resting, for enjoying the shade of a front porch, for rocking until the breeze ruffled your hair, whispered in your ear, reached down your neck and dried the sweat off your back. Watching the slow burn of sun on sand, Ruth would wait for a visitor or two. After the neighboring women had fixed their families' lunches and cleared away the plates, they'd be ready for an afternoon social. Meeting at one house on Monday, another on Tuesday, Ruth spent summer weekdays either hosting or visiting other women until the sun slouched over the Currituck, when each wife headed back to her own stuffy kitchen to set the table for supper.

On those summer afternoons, the women found chores light enough to carry along with them, projects they could share or tasks they could tackle sitting down. Maybe they brought some stitching to Ruth's front porch, a quilt for the coming winter, a fishing net that needed mending. They might have a basket of steamed crabs to pick or an apron filled with garden-grown pole beans for snapping. Camaraderie and conversation made every job simpler. After trading gossip, the women ex-changed stories about husbands and youngsters or, in later years, about grown children married and moved away, about their new grandbabies.

Until the early 1980s, Ruth knew the lay of this

THE HOUSE PICTURED HERE WAS TYPICAL OF THE HOMES FOUND IN DUCK IN
THE MID 1960s.
Courtesy of the Outer Banks History Center

land, every rising sand hill, every curve of sound front as familiar as her own children's features or the footsteps of friends climbing the porch steps. The house she lived in for forty years was situated in an area of the village that the county zoned commercial. Not so many years before, the property across the way had been known as Dog Corner, so named because packs of village mutts enjoyed dozing under the pines and oaks that grew there. Mostly mongrels, mottled and dopey-eyed, they were valued not for their breeding but for their obedient service, sometimes showing enough hound in them to sniff out dead ducks hidden in the marsh grass, sometimes catching and holding the hogs during roundups. Some dogs were lazy, flea-carrying nuisances that nosed around the yards for something to eat or a scratch between the ears. But each one had a name, and even if they didn't have a home to go to, they were never chased out of the village.

Those lost days of napping dogs and afternoons spent with neighborhood women had passed into folklore by the time Ruth witnessed the new "downtown" Duck flourishing around her. A few city journalists began to knock on her door or wait for her in the front yard. They wanted to hear about the "old times," which, to Ruth, didn't seem all that long ago.

On the other side of Duck Road, Scarborough Faire—more than a dozen specialty shops and eateries—filled the space that was once Dog Corner. Twiddy

Real Estate was another of Ruth's new neighbors. A second row of stores took root on the sandy lots between her yard and that of her double first cousin, Levin.

Ruth wasn't overly troubled by all the disturbances. Being prepared for the unexpected was a specialty of the old-timers, and Ruth had matured into a front-porch theorist. Her homespun wisdom came from years of examining the terrain around her. She had long ago met the wind that liked heaving sand from one place to another, witnessed tides and storm surges that cleaved out a piece of village one day, then gave back more than they had taken the next. There has always been a bit of the philosopher in most Duck natives, Ruth among them.

"You can't stop the world from moving on," she told a reporter in 1986. "It's going to move on with or without you, so you might as well make the best of it."

Ruth had seen the village change before, back in the 1940s, when World War II beckoned a new generation of Duck natives. They wandered away from the neighborhood, some traveling down Duck Road in uniform, ready to fight for the nation's cause in Europe or Asia. Others left in civilian clothes for jobs in shipbuilding or other wartime industries. Many never wandered back. Global discord and the lure of new economic opportunities affected Duck's population. From five hundred prewar residents, the village dwindled to less than a hundred by 1944.

Today, the population of Duck is steadily growing again. The only dogs you'll see along Duck Road are on leashes; the only hogs still found in the village are the ones already slaughtered, processed, and packaged as hot dogs. The leashed dogs look too pedigreed to consider chasing a hog or sniffing out a dead duck; each year, the hot dogs are harder and harder to find. Businesses in the village seem to cater more to upscale urbanites than homegrown locals.

As for Duck Road, Ruth eyed its advances farther and farther north. State work crews kept coming back, widening what they'd already paved, a few more inches of sandy soil deeded for the sake of progress and concealed under a layer of hot tar and asphalt. Then came more construction trucks, more realtors, more cars, more pedestrians, more shoppers, the bicyclists and the joggers, the kids on roller blades. Soon, clapboard shopping centers ranged like kudzu, growing along both sides of N.C. 12 until the buildings almost touched one another. But Ruth continued to experience the village as only she and a few others had known it. Hers was a distinctive vision, a particular acquaintance, a private verity. When she closed her eyes, she could still see the old faces, hear the old voices. She remembered the familiar greetings of old friends, the chorus of barks and growls, the mating calls that traveled through the night air from Dog Corner. She kept practicing the old ways—getting up early on summer mornings, finishing her chores, enjoying whatever pleasure the hot afternoons might bring to her front porch, keeping bad luck from sneaking over her doorstep after sundown.

"I don't feel no different from the way I always felt," Ruth said in the midst of the village's first growth spurt. "They can call Duck a village or a town or a community, whatever they want to call it. We called it 'the neighborhood,' and everybody here was just like one family."

❧❧❧

I'm sitting in a wooden booth at the Roadside Raw Bar and Grille, 1193 Duck Road. It's early on a March Tuesday; the restaurant is closed to customers until dinner. A few employees are stocking supplies or tidying up the back kitchen.

There's a folksy feel to this place, a rustic ambience, no glitz or sleek lines, nothing in cold metallic or sterile porcelain. Sun filters through the windows of the enclosed front porch. Soft jazz plays in the dining area. Across the room are a hooded grill with a silken finish, a cavernous oven, and an open kitchen for watching the preparation of main courses. Stacks of colored plates glisten on natural pine shelves. Near the front entrance, there's a homey bar with a half-dozen stools.

Ashley Copeland, the Roadside's manager and owner, comes down from her upstairs office. She's dressed in denim coveralls and a flannel shirt, layers of curly straw-colored hair framing a face as naturally pretty as the girl next door. She moves lightly, speaks quickly, offers me coffee, pours it from a pot behind the bar. She brings two mugs and sits down.

"This place was a private residence for a long time, one of the original Duck houses," she says, offering a cream pitcher. "In the last ten years, it's been a real-estate office and a surf shop. The garage used to be detached, and it was a developer's office. Now, it's our main dining room. We had to completely renovate this space once we took it over. It had been strictly retail, never a restaurant. We put a new roof on. There were at least eight coats of paint on this floor and a carpet glued on top of that. It took us forever to get it all off. But we eventually got down to the original hardwood. Then we got it to look the way it was supposed to."

M. J. Evans built this house. In April 1930, he found the elevated lot, probably imagined the view of the Currituck he'd have from an upstairs window, paid the $12.50 that J. K. and Lillian Hines asked for the land. Then the construction began. Two years later, Evans moved in. He'd dug the cellar out of the sand, joined the two stories with a plain pine staircase. Every floor-board was hand-cut, every wall put up to last, every exterior shingle sanded smooth as butter. It was all his doing, a carefully planned and crafted dwelling the villagers could admire. Evans made himself a fine-looking home for $250. Decades later, the floors haven't buckled, the ceilings don't slope, and the shingles have weathered a rich cappuccino. Now, a man named Neal Blinkin owns the property, the same half-acre lot and thousand square feet of structure valued at close to $400,000.

Copeland and her husband, Mark, began leasing the building from Blinkin in January 1995. Mark completed all the repairs and did the reconditioning himself before they opened the doors to customers five months later.

"I'd already been in Duck for a while, about fifteen years, before we opened the Roadside," Ashley says. "I started coming down during the summers in the early '80s, when I was in college. Met Mark the very first night I was here. He was from Florida and on his way to California. He'd stopped on the Outer Banks to do some surfing."

Originally from Greensboro, North Carolina, Copeland graduated from Elon College with a double major in English and philosophy. Everything she knows about the restaurant business she learned from on-the-job experience.

"Mark lived in Duck when I met him, in a little house across the street from Wee Winks, where the Lady Victorian is now. That first summer, I stayed in Kitty Hawk and got a job as a cocktail waitress up here at the Barrier Island. It had only been open a year. Mark ended up staying in Duck because there was so much building going on down here then. That's what he still does. I finished school, we got married, and here we are. We just decided to stay."

Copeland resolved to open a restaurant of her own after working at the Blue Point, another eatery in the village. "I helped open that place," she says. "I watched everything the owners did, and I started thinking 'Hmm, this is something I need to be doing as well.' When this property became available, we jumped on it. We'd been looking for a few years. That's the hardest part of opening something in Duck, finding the right place."

The Roadside's interior is close and cozy. Only one level is used for the restaurant. The two dining rooms include three booths, seven tables, and six barstools, for a seating capacity of only thirty-six. During the summer, Copeland might be here seven days a week, twelve hours a day, whether ordering supplies and doing paperwork in her upstairs office or helping to keep things moving downstairs. She might be the hostess who greets you at the door or the woman busing your table, filling your water glass, or slicing your bread in the kitchen.

In season, the flow of lunch customers usually begins at eleven. The last diners sometimes don't leave until almost midnight. When the weather is good, Copeland sets out tables and umbrellas on the front patio. It's the Roadside's alfresco bar, where patrons can sip imported beer and drink in the view or browse a menu and the daily specials. No one seems to mind the wait; the word around the village is that the Roadside serves the best crab cakes on the North Banks.

"Our first season was pretty good," Copeland says, "but it was a first season. Now, things are great. Used to be, we would shut down for a few months in the off-season. But the off-season is getting shorter and shorter every winter. We were closed for about four weeks in January this year. I'm not sure if we'll close at all next year. Year-round, there are more people down here all the time. The population has grown. More homeowners come down in the off-season—more vacationers, too.

"Before I opened the Roadside, I might not have liked all the growth. I think it bothers some of the residents in Duck. You know, part of *me* still wants to be the last one over the bridge and then burn it behind me. But if that were the way things had happened in Duck, I wouldn't be here. I wouldn't have this business.

"Things change around here all the time. Duck has always been changing. When I first got down here, the Ship's Watch development was just going up and the Barrier Island condominiums were just about finished. Across the street from where Schooner Ridge is now, there was this big sand trap. That's where we used to go to the beach. Places like the Barrier Island Restaurant, they were before their time. You couldn't buy liquor by the drink in Duck back then, only beer and wine. And it wasn't busy. There weren't many people around. Now, I have customers filling this place every night from Easter till Halloween. Thanksgiving weekend is just like a summer weekend, and the weeks around the Christmas holidays are getting pretty hectic. I've already had calls about reservations for next New Year's Eve. It's crazy."

Some folks probably thought Mark and Ashley were a trifle crazy when they found out the couple was planning to open a restaurant in the old Evans place. Every other business occupying this house had failed after a few years.

Ashley laughs. "People said it couldn't be done, but I always thought this place would work. The restaurant has come a long way since the first year. I've got a really great chef and a really great staff. There are seven people on my core crew, and I pick up extra folks to work during the summers. I tell my staff to concentrate on hospitality. I guess I sort of drill it into them. For the most part, our customers are working people. They spend fifty-one weeks a year doing the nine-to-five. For one week, they come to Duck because they think it's a paradise. If they choose to splurge on a big night out at the Roadside, I think we owe them something. We need to be especially gracious.

"We're not just a tourist spot. We get people from the neighborhood eating here. Frank and Sue Scarborough come for dinner. Gary and Theresa Scarborough will stop in for a drink. The folks that work at Kellogg's Supply have lunch over here all the time."

Copeland checks her watch. A working mother with two children, she needs to finish a few things before she leaves to pick her youngest up from preschool.

"It's always been really hard to make a living down here," she says. "Most people have to work two or three jobs just to survive. You've got to look at all this progress with that in mind. People have families to raise, and this growth is the only thing that will give them the opportunity to do it."

She admits that she's not sure how well her restaurant would have worked if it were located in a new section of the village. "I think our being in an original Duck house really sets us apart," she says. "It's very appealing to most visitors, and the natives seem to like it, too. It's more personal than eating in a shopping center or some building that has just sprung up. We're a part of the neighborhood."

❧❧❧

Tom Blanchard remembers when Duck Road went past the village line toward Corolla.

"That's when I'd say things really started changing around here," he says. A native of Elizabeth City, Blanchard now lives on the Outer Banks and owns a small but lucrative chain of hardware stores spread out between Duck and Manteo.

In the 1950s, as a teenager, Blanchard traveled to Duck every now and then, mostly on weekends. He and a few friends came to the village at night. They'd search the stretch of beach owned by the United States government, where the navy bombing range used to be. "We'd look for those old smoke bombs," he says. "They were the only souvenirs anyone could take home from Duck back then."

Forty years later, Blanchard visits Duck regularly to check on his business, Kellogg's Supply Company. The store is situated on a slope of land facing the sound, on the eastern side of Duck Road. From inside the main entrance, a shopper could admire the Currituck if it weren't for the thick foliage interrupting the view. Blanchard decided to buy this sizable tract of land— now divided among his store, Christopher Drive, and the Centura Bank—on September 5, 1984. During that year, Duck's population almost doubled.

Blanchard uses the Manteo store as his headquarters. His office is spacious and tidy. He keeps the surveyors' diagrams of his Duck property in the middle drawer of a filing cabinet. He locates them so quickly it seems as though he has just closed the deal. I almost expect the ink on the seals to be a little moist as he spreads the documents over the top of his executive desk.

"Let's see," Blanchard says, handing me copies of the surveyors' work. "I know I bought a piece from a man named Gravely, a small piece." On the diagram, Blanchard identifies a triangular lot measuring 11,150 square feet, originally titled to a P. K. Gravely.

Blanchard wears the years of midlife well. He has the polish of an Ivy Leaguer and the vitality of a sportsman. It's easy to imagine him behind a lectern or on a playing field; maybe he's a weekend camper or the Saturday skipper of a sloop. Tall, trim, and well conditioned, he has a youthful grin and a good tan, though it's still the middle of winter. There's a tinge of gray in his hair, and he never has to reach far for the pair of reading glasses he needs to scrutinize the small print and faint lines on the surveyors' diagrams. But Blanchard still looks as if he could sail a football fifty yards or make a jump shot from the foul line. He has a loose, casual style, as befits a businessman who prefers khaki slacks and an open-neck sweater to a suit and tie.

"The biggest portion I purchased belonged to R. D. Sawyer. He owned that piece," Blanchard says, pointing on the sheet to a 1.84-acre parcel with the name *R. D. Sawyer Motor Company* nicely centered and printed in neat block letters. This oddly shaped section of Blanchard's property looks like a geometrical hybrid between a rectangle and a triangle, with just a touch of parabola on its western edge.

"This last piece, another small one, I bought from the Four Seasons Resort," Blanchard continues. "It was only a little piece, about eighty-two hundred square feet. That's all." An earlier surveyor's diagram, this one done in 1980, documents that the Four Seasons tract was once the property of S. A. Thomas.

At first, Blanchard recalls the land as unexceptional. Then he raises his head, and his eyes brighten a little, a smile deepening the creases around his eyes. "Except," he says, "for this incredible stand of live oak." That stand, Blanchard explains, grew down the middle of his combined parcels. "I had three different buildings designed to try and preserve those oaks, but I just couldn't do it, and eventually, I had to have each one of them taken down." His voice is low; the smile has disappeared. "I really did try to save them."

Blanchard itemizes what he found on the site that is now the Duck store. "Ah, yes," he says with a soft chuckle, "there was an old, rusted-out school bus on the lot, and I recall that they picked up a good deal of wood and trash when they cleaned up the land. Must have been what was left of an old house."

His Duck store has grown and flourished. On any morning, whether in season or not, the parking lot is crowded with construction-company pickups and painters' panel vans. Summer visitors shop at Kellogg's, too. They browse through stacks of *Duck* ball caps and T-shirts, search the racks of silk ties with tiny tennis rackets, minuscule fish, or Outer Banks lighthouses printed on them. Twin carousels with souvenir key chains and greeting cards spin near the front entrance, not far from the barbecue grills and paintbrushes. For beach lovers, there are high-backed sand chairs, for campers, canvas dome tents. Tow ropes in a variety of lengths and widths attract boaters. Dog owners seem drawn to a new selection of designer pet collars and leashes across the aisle from the anvils and bow saws.

Those owning rental properties often wander through the store in the off-season. On winter Saturdays, customers fill shopping carts with all the paraphernalia they'll need for repairs and cosmetic touch-ups. Having originally intended Kellogg's Supply as a lumber and building-materials pickup point for construction companies during Duck's growth spurt in the mid-1980s, Blanchard has added summer furnishings, pottery, exotic plants, fine linens, wallpaper, kitchen utensils, interior and exterior decorations. There are decorative and American flags, at least two dozen kinds of wind chimes, wall clocks, and hand-painted barometers. And like every store in Duck, there are a few shelves reserved for suntan oils and lotions.

Within the last few years, Blanchard's Duck store has adopted a new motto to go along with its new clientele. A red banner hanging above the doorway reads, "As Usual . . . the Unusual."

☽☽☽

Adjoining the Currituck across Duck Road from Kellogg's Supply is a deep lot overgrown with parched brown brush as tall as trees. There's a gray mailbox with *1196* stenciled on the side and the name *Townsend* spelled out in black metal letters across the top. Next to the lot in a clearing set back from the road stands an aging house, one and a half stories of buckling, blistered, salt-stained shingles topped with an aluminum roof. Concrete blocks form a foundation, pairs of them wedged under corners. Others serve as steps and prop up the porch floor, a rippled row of bare boards too fragile to hold much weight.

Someone has pulled the shades in the two front windows. The front door probably hasn't been opened in months. The only sign of life is a single green vine, this chain of ivy rising through a hole in the porch floor. Already, it has climbed the torn screens, curved around the dented doorknob, crept over the rusted latches and peeling doorframe. In another few weeks, it will probably be tangled around the rafters of the porch roof.

Across the yard, there are no barriers, neither a picket nor a wire fence to keep visitors out. Nothing has been tilled, no ground turned over for spring planting, no evidence of there ever having been a garden at all. Furniture weathers under an eave on the side porch—a few decaying chairs, a warped picnic table, a whitewashed cupboard, a splintered oak bench, a peeling church pew, a bureau bleached the color of sand. Around back, there's a brick chimney. A tulip-shaped light fixture harvests rust and spider webs. Six feet of water pipe cling to the shingles like a metal snake with a spigot for a head. Lanky weeds sway in one corner; in another, a white commode leans on its side, as if napping.

It's a bright day, the sky clear, the air mellow with the promise of spring. The turf is stiff and low, maybe mowed at the end of the last summer season and stunted by a winter frost. Along the edge of the property, in the space where the lawn meets the asphalt, the former residents of this house lie buried side by side. Emerson and Maryland Rodgers, Emerson's brother Johnnie, and two of the couple's three children, Charlie and Harriet, flank the lot like sleeping sentinels. Only a few feet separate their headstones from Duck Road. Sprays of coarse grass divide their graves.

"Seems as if just about everyone who originally lived in that house is buried in the front yard," Brack Townsend says. Townsend is talking to me on the phone from his home in Rocky Mount. His father, Braxton, now deceased, bought the old Rodgers house more than thirty years ago with his friend Charles Wheless. Now, Brack's mother, Ellen, and Wheless's son, Charles, Jr., own the property.

"I don't go down much anymore," Brack Townsend says. "It's too crowded, and the traffic is terrible. My son spent a summer in that house three years ago, and my nephew stayed there last summer. My family's been going to Duck for a long time. We always lived in Rocky Mount, but we'd go there to fish, mainly bass. Later on, we did some duck hunting."

Townsend's recollections go back to the 1950s, when he spent winter and summer vacations at Sand-

erling, in the area where the Caffey's Inlet Coast Guard
Station used to be.

"There were five houses that had been built for the
men stationed there. After they moved out, we owned
one of those houses, but not the land it was built on.
We had to lease it from a Currituck gun club. When

Earl Slick bought all that land, he wouldn't renew the lease, so we had to abandon the Caffey house. We couldn't move it.

"After that, my family bought the Rodgers place, and then Daddy bought the six or seven acres next to it. The house had been abandoned. My father did some research on the ownership of it. None of the surviving heirs wanted it because it had what was called an old-age lend on it. Apparently, the Rodgerses borrowed money from the government to live on. They must have used the house as collateral, but they never could pay the loan back."

The Rodgers family's financial troubles seem to have started early. In the mid-1920s, Emerson bought three-fourths of an acre of wooded sound front from a man named Abner Leary. By 1928, Emerson and Maryland must have been facing foreclosure. Turning to kin for help, they relinquished their ownership—but not their possession—of the lot and the house they'd built on it.

According to the deed, William Rogers—his surname spelled differently and his relationship to Emerson unclear—paid $150 in exchange for a triangular piece of property "beginning at a Gum tree on the main road [and] running a westerly course across a branch or swamp." Presumably, the arrangement included William's settling the original mortgage. No longer threatened by bank officials, Emerson and Maryland found themselves indebted to him, not figuratively but literally. In addition to the taxes, they agreed to pay William the principal—an undisclosed amount—in monthly installments until the note was satisfied. He charged them interest at a rate of 6 percent. E. W. Baum, a notary in Dare County, witnessed Emerson and Maryland as each one scratched an **X** on the lines above their names.

Whatever the Rodgers family lacked in income and education, they made up for with religion, their front and side porches the site of many revivals. On the Sabbath, someone from the village or the mainland might be baptized in the water behind their house. Often, an itinerant preacher ate at their table. Maryland, known to her neighbors as "Med," would always prepare enough chicken and dumplings or fried fish and boiled potatoes to fill, and refill, the plates of a visiting minister and his wife.

They seemed a guileless couple, Emerson and Med, the thirty-three years they spent together in Duck memorable mainly for the losses they suffered, the hardships they endured, the faith they clung to, the home they struggled to keep. Emerson had two occupations, most often working as a fisherman but moonlighting as a carpenter whenever jobs were available. Med was a modest woman, never venturing out the door unless she was covered from head to toe. She wore a wide-brimmed felt hat and ankle-length dresses even when styles and temperatures dictated otherwise. If the wind was up and she needed to mend a net for her husband, Med would stitch lead weights into the hem of her skirt before she left the house. No one but Emerson ever saw much above her shoes, certainly nothing as high as her calves.

In 1930, while the Depression was making its way from the mainland to the North Banks, Emerson and Med managed to hold on to their property. But in mid-May of that year, they lost their only daughter, Harriet, four months shy of her thirteenth birthday. Her grave was the first one Emerson dug in the front yard. Eight months later, Emerson's brother Johnnie, twenty-nine, was crushed by a falling tree; they buried him in a plot on Harriet's right side. Six years passed before their twenty-three-year-old son, Charlie, died and was laid to rest on Harriet's left. A second son, Willie, likewise died young, but they buried him in one of the village cemeteries.

For the next twenty years, the couple lived alone, just two places set at the table, just two rockers on the front porch, just one bed occupied at night. Med died first, in 1957, leaving Emerson with no family but a brother in Wanchese and a sister in Aydlett. Perhaps it had already been agreed that, like Charlie and Harriet, Emerson and Med would spend eternity in their own front yard. Marking a space for himself before he buried Med, Emerson probably prepared for the day when he would lie down beside her.

After a suitable period of mourning, Emerson, then seventy-five, decided to look for a second wife. He found a lonely woman, Lilly Meekins, already widowed and the mother of a grown son. Emerson had heirs again. Overnight, he went from a solitary, childless widower to a husband, stepfather, and granddaddy of seven. Lilly moved into Emerson's house. She cooked meals in Med's pots, cleaned the outhouse in Med's backyard, filled the void left on Med's side of the bed.

By the end of 1960, Emerson's heart was weakening. Maybe it was a winter flu or a pinch of pleurisy that drained what strength he had. Having nursed Emerson through other bouts of bad health, Lilly may have worried that this sick spell differed from the others. But she never forced Emerson to leave the house, never called an ambulance to take him across the Currituck to a mainland hospital in Elizabeth City or Norfolk. On a Tuesday afternoon, January 3, 1961, Emerson stopped breathing. Lilly let him die where he wanted to, at home in Duck.

Three days later, just before two o'clock, the Reverend Woody Barnes knocked on the door of the Rodgers house. He carried a dog-eared Bible in his pocket and words of condolence on his tongue. He extended his hand in sympathy. Lilly let him in first. Then she opened the door to the other mourners waiting on the porch for the service to begin.

Emerson's funeral was held in the parlor, his

survivors and village neighbors all crowded into a single room. The Reverend Barnes leading them, they sang the opening hymn, listened to the Psalms Lilly had chosen and the sermon about the scarcity of material wealth Emerson had found on earth and the treasures that waited for him in heaven.

After the final prayer and song, Emerson's pallbearers carried his plain pine coffin out the front door, over a few feet of porch, and down the two unsteady steps. It was drizzling by then, a prickling rain that would freeze by nightfall. Already, the earth felt hard, and the gum tree glistened. After a short procession through the yard, they lowered Emerson into the grave he'd chosen for himself four years before. He'd spend the hereafter next to Med along the edge of Duck Road.

Lilly Meekins Rodgers died three years and three days after Emerson. From January 6, 1964, the date of Lilly's death, to April 21, 1967, when Braxton Townsend purchased it, the house remained vacant.

"I couldn't believe my father even considered buying that place," Townsend says. "But there wasn't anything much else down there to buy. It was very remote then. Only two houses stood between us and the beach. There was nothing but a huge dune across the way. We had an old Jeep truck we used to drive over it. It was a clear shot all the way to the ocean.

"I was a teenager the first time I saw that house, and it looked so bad I didn't think it was fixable. There was no kitchen, no bathroom. Pigeons were roosting inside. It had an outdoor john in the yard, no running water, just a well with a pump. All the windows had been broken out. Somebody must have gone in there thinking they could steal some money. They had torn all the mattresses and pillows upstairs. The place was knee deep in feathers and broken green glass. The floors had holes in them. People must have dumped their garbage and left their trash in there. The entire yard was completely covered in briars and brambles. It wasn't livable—just awful.

"Across the street from us, about where Kellogg's Hardware is now, there was a native Duckian by the name of Willie Hines. He lived in a little white house with his wife. Her name was Sue, but Willie never called her that. He introduced her to everyone as "Wyrff," so that's what we called her, Wyrff Hines. Willie was an amazing character, a tiny, wiry guy with the most incredible look in his eye. He was all mischief.

"Willie was pretty much like most of the people down there then. They all lived off the land. He had been a fisherman. Until we met him, we'd only fished in the sound. He showed us how to put nets out in the ocean. He had worked as a guide for the men who used to go down there to duck hunt, and I think he had put a few blinds of his own out in the sound. He kept all kinds of animals in his yard, had a couple of wild boars in a pen. He let the chickens, pigs, and goats just wander around, and he raised pigeons.

"After Daddy bought the Rodgers place, Willie helped us out a lot. He took the goats from his house across the road, tethered them, and let them stay until they'd eaten out a huge circle. It was the only way we could get into our yard. Willie's goats cleared that whole piece of property.

"I never knew too much about the Rodgers family, never heard too much about them except for what Willie told us. I remember his saying that Emerson's wife was so lonely for him after he died, she sat on the front porch all day with the door wide open and the radio turned up full blast. Guess she wanted Emerson to hear the music.

"We started using the house in the late '60s. It was still nice and quiet in Duck. There was mighty little growth back then. Nobody wanted that land. Everything in Duck took off very slowly, and then all of a sudden, sometime around the late '70s and early '80s, everything went crazy. But in 1969, maybe there was one or two developments just starting up. Of course, Southern Shores was already there, but once you got north of it on Duck Road, there wasn't anything but dunes full of sea oats and myrtle.

"There were woods just as you came into the village, then a little house on the right-hand side. Andrew Scarborough and his family lived there. Around the big curve, there were probably five or six more houses.

Mr. Santos—he was from Portugal—lived in one of them. He was probably the only person in Duck back then with a foreign accent. He was a real nice fella, very friendly. Everybody liked him. He used to say that he had come ashore on a board. That's what everybody believed, that he'd been shipwrecked somewhere south of Duck, washed up on the beach, and stayed. He was a good guy, a good fisherman. Pop Scarborough and the Tates were there then, too. Up a dirt road across from the Scarboroughs' place, they had a trailer park. The Beal brothers lived north of Willie's, in a house just a little way past where the Centura Bank is now. It was a pretty rough place—no running water, a johnny house outside. They had no shower, and they didn't smell too good, but they showed my daddy how to gill-net fish in the sound. Sinclair Beal, one of the brothers, had a pretty serious drinking problem. He'd fish until he had some money, then he'd start drinking. It wouldn't be long before he was drunk, and everybody who saw him would say 'Lord, Sinclair's ridin' the pig again.'

"The old Duck Methodist Church was just up the road past our house. It was a pretty place, a little white clapboard building. On Easter, the church members would hide eggs all over our property down there, around the house and behind it going back to the sound. The village kids would search back there for hours. Maybe there were twenty-five houses in Duck by 1970. Maybe Wee Winks was there, too, but it was about a third of the size it is now. Just beyond the church is where the paved road used to end. About a half-mile north of there, the road went down along the water until you got to where the Sound Sea development is today. I think there was only one house along there then.

"What I most remember about Duck back then is Willie. He did most of the work on the Rodgers house after Daddy bought it. Willie was a real pack rat. He had stuff stockpiled around either side and behind his house. Back then, if you went to the beach after a storm, you could find all sorts of things. Willie would come back with timber that had broken off boats, rough-cut mahogany boards they used for packing crates on ships from Africa. He put down a new porch floor for us. It was all mahogany. It looked good, but it rotted easily. He already had a collection of odd doors and windows, all sorts of wood. He patched the walls, helped us get a kitchen put together and do some wiring. It was Willie who really put that house back together for us."

Years later, when the Hines house burned down, Townsend's father and a couple of his friends from Rocky Mount repaid Willie and Sue's kindnesses. They bought a trailer for them to live in until the couple decided what they wanted to do. Willie eventually sold his property in Duck, and he and Sue moved to the mainland. "He got fifty thousand dollars for it and thought he was rich," Townsend says. "He and Sue left Duck, but that trailer they lived in is still behind our house down there."

When Willie relocated to the mainland, he left more behind than the trailer the men from Rocky Mount gave him. Almost forty years later, Townsend can still mimic Willie's voice. He chuckles about Willie's colorful charisma and his audacious repartee. "I can't think of Willie without remembering the crazy stories he used to tell. Some of them I wouldn't repeat. A lot of times, they'd be about the hurricanes he'd seen come through Duck or shipwrecks he'd seen on the beach. The men, my daddy and the others, they'd all go to Willie's front porch after they'd gone hunting or fishing and purposely get him going.

"This one time, they were all sitting around Willie's place after they'd been out fishing. Willie was talking about how good things were in Duck even when times looked bad, how he'd always had plenty to eat. 'Can always shoot me a white turkey for Christmas,' Willie said. 'Good eatin'. I like swan on the holidays.'

"'What does swan taste like?' one of the men asked.

"'It's *goood*, all white meat, tastes a lot like chicken.'

"'Ya ever eaten possum?' another man asked.

"'Sure,' Willie said, 'I've eat possum. It's greasy. Tastes a little like pork, just greasier.'

"'What about a raccoon?'

"'Yeah, had raccoon, but coons are pretty tough. Taste somethin' like squirrel.'

"'You eaten squirrel, too, Willie?'

"'Yeah, had plenty of squirrel. Sweeter than coon or possum. Taste a little like rabbit.'

"'Eat a lot of rabbit, Willie?'

"'Yeah, plenty of rabbit. Lot easier to chew than bear.'

"'Willie, you had yourself a bear?'

"'Sure, I've had myself a bear. Tastes a lot like fox.'

"'You like fox, Willie?'

"'Yeah, fox is okay. Tastes a lot like *dawg*.'"

Last year, Ken Forlano took no orders for swan or fox, but he did serve more than two tons of smoked pork barbecue at the Duck Deli, the family-owned eatery he's been operating with his father, Ron, at 1378 Duck Road since 1987.

"My dad has always been a true entrepreneur," Ken says. "He retired from dentistry at forty-nine, moved down here from Pennsylvania, and started out selling commercial real estate. Then this place came across his desk. When he saw it was for sale, he knew it would be a good buy for him. He always had it earmarked for me and my older brother, Chris, to run."

Ken is dressed in a T-shirt and jeans. He's not as tall as most professional athletes, but his shoulders are every bit as broad as an NFL lineman's. He has an affable expression, close-cut hair, and dark eyes. He's quick to smile, has perfect teeth and an easy laugh. He offers me something to drink, carries the soda in one hand and a portable phone in the other.

Ken was twenty-one and had just graduated from Ryder College in New Jersey with a degree in business and computers. He had visions of a corporate career, was polishing his resume, trying on three-piece suits, contacting headhunters, studying the classifieds in Sunday papers. Then his father called.

"Ken," he said, "how would you like to work down here in Duck, open a deli with me?"

"What do we know about running a deli?" Ken asked.

"Nothing, but we'll learn."

Ken didn't spend much time deliberating before he

THE DUCK DELI, A FAMILY-OWNED EATERY, HAS BEEN LOCATED ON DUCK ROAD SINCE 1987.
Courtesy of Peter J. Mercier, III

accepted his father's offer. He liked the idea of being his own boss. *Okay*, he thought, *I'll go down there, check it out, work a year, maybe two, get some management experience, and be on my merry way.* Eleven years later, Ken is still inventing recipes and new ways to expand the family business.

As a teenager, he had a string of part-time jobs in restaurants, mostly sub and pizza places up north. By college, he was wearing an apron and standing over a stove in an Italian restaurant. "I knew how to operate a kitchen," Ken says. "It was the business side of it I didn't know. I made a lot of mistakes when I first started out. I had a lot to learn."

Today, Ken started cooking at six in the morning. It's just after three, the lunch crowd gone, the deli closing early. It's the off-season. Two of his wait staff take charge of prepping the deli for tomorrow's opening. One sweeps the floor; the other fills the condiment trays on the counter and polishes the glass case.

The Forlano family started coming to Duck in 1974 for family vacations. Ken's uncle, a navy pilot, was the first to spy Duck. While stationed at Oceana Air Base in Virginia, he flew practice runs over the village's bombing range. Now, Ken's uncle is retired and owns a house in Southern Shores.

"My parents always picked these really remote spots to take me and my three brothers," Ken says. "Twenty-five years ago, this place was one of them. None of this was here. There was no such thing as a rental house back then. We used to camp in a trailer park on what's now Scarborough Lane. After my grandparents retired, they moved up here from Augusta, Georgia. My dad followed. Now, here I am."

In a few days, another Forlano will be relocating to Duck. Ken's youngest brother, Brian, and his wife have agreed to help Ken run the deli. "As soon as they get here, I'll have my night staff," he says. "We're a family-run operation, and experience down here has taught me that nobody does it better than your family."

Like the Roadside, Duck Deli is small, quaint, comfortable. A white clapboard cottage facing Duck Road, it has a simple design and an open front deck that is dwarfed by a backdrop of stately oaks and pines. Resting at the foot of a hill leading to the Saltaire subdivision, Ken's restaurant is no original Duck home, but it does stand in an area of the village now zoned residential.

"There's a lot of hostility toward me as a businessman because of the zoning situation," Ken says. "Basically, the original owners moved this building here in 1982. They literally plunked this place down and began doing business in a residential zone. It started out as a furniture store and then evolved into a deli. Of course, back then, it didn't seem like such a big deal, but now some residents are really pissed off about it. They're angry about what happened fifteen years ago. When I moved down here, the deli was already here, and I just went along with it, but I've inherited that old anger."

It was 1976 when some Duck villagers decided they would no longer dawdle. They had a vision for their community's future, and they weren't sure they liked what they saw coming. That spring, a six-year zoning skirmish began. Blanch Utz, a longtime resident, fired the first shot, circulating a petition that read, "We, the undersigned, residents or property owners of Duck, would like zoning as soon as possible." She carried it to Manteo and presented it to the Dare County Board of Commissioners with thirty-one signatures.

About the same time, another group of concerned citizens in Duck circulated a second petition. This one, which had almost twice as many signatures as Blanch's, opposed *any* zoning restrictions for the village. Even members of the same families couldn't agree: some Scarboroughs advocated limits; other Scarboroughs deplored them.

Many names on the anti-zoning petition belonged to Duck's oldest natives—Levin and Elsie Scarborough, the Beal brothers, Ruth Tate. Their resistance to government intervention was as fierce in the 1970s as it had been decades earlier, when bans on the open grazing of livestock and game limits on wild waterfowl had endangered their economic survival. To some of Duck's old-timers, inviting county officials to nose around their neighborhood was as good as asking for trouble.

A year later, Duck had its first five-member citizens' committee, among whose members were Blanch Utz and two Scarboroughs. They pressed for zoning. By November 9, 1977, the county designed a map that sliced up Duck like a cadaver. Vertical lines here, horizontal lines there, rectangles and squares, every inch of the village marked with one of five codes—single-family residential, medium-density residential, neighborhood commercial, village commercial, and special district. Blanch hung the map in Wee Winks for public examination.

Within ten days, the Dare County Board of Commissioners office was swamped with letters from Duck, most of them voicing disapproval. Two years later, after a series of canceled and rescheduled public meetings and a stack of revised maps, the villagers could agree only on minimal zoning, what the county called "S-1," a code that permitted all uses and served mainly as a guide for parking, set-backs, heights, densities, and lot coverage. Duck would be a developer's paradise. Just about anything could be built just about anywhere.

By 1982, a greater number of villagers favored stricter zoning laws. Conditions in Duck called for new action. Once again, they approached the county for help. This time, they requested that a moratorium be placed on high-density development, their immediate concerns stemming from the condominiums and time shares that threatened to weigh down the oceanfront.

But the county was impotent. Without a comprehensive zoning plan for Duck, there could be no moratorium. The condos went up; the time shares opened. The zoning process would have to start all over again.

Within days, ten Duck residents volunteered to be members of a study committee. They'd look for consensus, get a feel for what the villagers wanted, report their findings to Manteo, try giving everyone a say in the plan. There was a public meeting in May, another in June. By July, Duck had a comprehensive zoning plan just about everyone could agree on.

With the new zoning regulations came a new land-use classification—nonconforming or special use. Duck Deli is one such property, a commercial building situated in a residentially zoned area. The designation allows the Forlanos to continue operating the business, but it restricts their ability to expand or alter the deli's exterior contours. If a hurricane should wash the deli away or a bolt of lightning ignite it, Ken would be out of luck. He couldn't rebuild the business on his Duck Road site.

"I was at a planning meeting not too long ago," Ken says, his head already shaking at the thought of it. "And a woman there asked me when I was going to stop being a deli. I looked her in the eye and said, 'Never.' Don't think I don't know how hoppin' happy some of my neighbors would be if this place burned down, and that scares me. I've become a very careful businessman.

I've done just about everything I can to ensure that this place is fireproof."

The Forlanos made several attempts to alter the zoning for their Duck Road deli, but they never met with any success, only resistance.

"There was so much animosity, we just stopped trying," Ken says. "The folks that fight us the most are afraid of change. They're scared of growth. They think all growth, any growth, is bad. To me, they're fighting the wrong enemy—the small family-run businesses like this one—but they're losing the bigger battle."

Despite the zoning restrictions and the enmity Ken senses from some of his neighbors, Duck has been good to him. "I kind of feel honored that I'm here after eleven years," he says. "This can be a pretty rugged place to live year-round. I've seen a lot of people come and go. Businesses seem to change hands every six months, every season, especially restaurants. But this is where my family is. This is where my wife, Sharon, and I plan raising our four kids. It's a simple life.

"Sure, I have limitations here, but I can't fight that. This will be just fine. I can make a good living here. Running this deli is like breathing air to me. I'm staying here forever, regardless of what happens. I can't see ever going back to where I'm from. I've finally found what I want. It's a beautiful place."

Ken concedes that over the last decade, he, too, has found some of the changes in Duck discouraging.

"The fishing's gotten worse," he says with a chuckle.

"When I first moved down here, there wasn't much, and everything that was here was privately owned. Tommy Graves owned Tommy's Market; he'd built it, made it, but then he sold it. Herron's Deli was here, another family-run business, but I hear that might be going out soon. Wee Winks, that was here a long time ago, but who knows how long they'll survive?

"Seems as if things might be headed corporate these days. That's what I mean about some of the residents fighting the wrong cause and losing the real battle. Problem is, no one seems to know what they want Duck to look like in twenty years, and that's bad. If you have no vision for the future, then all the growth just happens hodgepodge. Somebody will squeeze this in here, that in there. When you let that sort of business growth happen, you're doomed. You've given yourself over to corporate steamrollers.

"I have no doubt that steamroller is just waiting to plow through a place like Duck. And once you go corporate, there's no going back. It's their symbols, their signs, their way. To me, that's about the worst sort of change that can happen here. If we let it, Duck will never be the same."

VII

Dennis
and
Other
Menaces

As I write this, Hurricane Floyd swirls in the Atlantic, already a category 3 storm. Forecasters anticipate it will probably gain strength before taking a northwesterly course toward the eastern seaboard of the United States. Though it's too early to predict landfall with any surety, experts warn that Floyd could collide with the coast of Florida or venture farther north like the last hurricane, Dennis, which, after being downgraded to a tropical storm, loitered in the waters off the Outer Banks for nearly a week.

An aerial view of the construction of the Duck water tower
shows a view of the village prior to development.
Courtesy of the Outer Banks History Center

Less than ten days ago, Dennis dashed the barrier-island beachfront. Waves at the Army Corps of Engineers' research pier in Duck measured thirteen feet above normal. Bullying winds stripped sand off the frontal dunes and deposited more than six inches of it onto roadways in Kitty Hawk and Kill Devil Hills. A mix of ocean overwash and pelting rains submerged a section of N.C. 12 on Hatteras Island between Avon and Buxton, stranding residents and making evacuation impossible. No lives were lost and no serious injuries reported, but Dennis proved a destructive and expensive visitor. Dare County authorities estimate recovery costs in the millions.

For the most part, Duck escaped the fury of Dennis, suffering far less physical damage than its neighboring communities farther south. But all major storms come here as thieves, especially when they arrive near a summer holiday weekend. For seven days, Dennis filched a portion of Duck's beachfront, the plunging, spilling breakers dragging truckloads of sand out to sea. Lifting realtors' and merchants' revenues like a pickpocket, Dennis canceled vacation plans, kept the tourists away. The rain-soaked houses remained vacant before Labor Day, the restaurants and specialty shops silent as cloisters.

Now, as villagers await news of a second hurricane seething in the Atlantic, they prepare for another sort of menace ready to encroach upon Duck. This threat comes with no wind, no waves, no rain. It approaches from the mainland.

Rumors began floating through the village in early March: Virginia developers were courting a nationally known grocery chain. They had their sights on the only remaining piece of the Currituck Sound front left in the commercially zoned area of Duck.

"Have you heard the latest?" Ron Forlano was the first to ask me. "A new store is coming to Duck, probably Food Lion. Can you believe it? They plan to build right next to the Herron Deli, in the vacant lot there. First Burger King, now this. Duck doesn't seem like a *village* anymore."

In April, the subject of a corporate-owned grocery store on the Currituck came up again, this time with Nancy Caviness, a member of the Duck Civic Commission. My husband, Peter, and I were spending a wet weekend at Advice 5 Cents, the bed-and-breakfast that Caviness and Donna Black, two native Upstate New Yorkers, have owned and operated on Scarborough Lane since 1995. It was early on a Sunday morning, and Nancy, an avid runner and accomplished baker, was warming up. She wore a loose-fitting pair of jogging shorts and a T-shirt, moved around the gourmet kitchen as if it were a track, her performance unhampered by apron or oven mitts. The house usually smelled of juniper but was now scented with ripe fruit, a touch of citrus, a hint of vanilla. Donna carried baskets of

Nancy's cranberry-lemon scones and peach muffins through the door. Nancy followed right behind her with the coffee, first filling our cups, then those of the middle-aged couple from Washington, D.C., who had just sat down at the table. Between spoonfuls of kiwi and strawberries, we talked about the tempestuous weather.

"One northeaster after another," Donna said. "It's been that way down here most of the spring."

Rattling the windows and shaking the walls, a fierce blast interrupted our chatter. The lights flickered. In deferential silence, we watched the wind chase the rain in circles outside the house.

"I don't mind the water," Donna said. "It washes all that salty film off the glass."

An hour later, while we drained a third pot of coffee and nibbled our way through a second round of scones and muffins, the storm intensified and the conversation evolved. Talk of Duck's messy weather seemed to lead us naturally into a discussion of some recently conceived businesses. We agreed that Duck was losing its village flavor. We complained about the crowds and commercialism on Duck Road and about how the new Burger King and two-island Chevron station made unseemly neighbors for the old white clapboard Methodist church. Soon, the rumored Food Lion was the talk of the table.

At the mention of it, the couple from D.C. frowned.

"What do they need a Food Lion here for?" the woman asked. "I saw a big one right down the road."

From the kitchen doorway, Nancy gently admonished us for our presumptions. "It's not *definite*," she said. "It's not a done deal just yet."

In late February 1999, the Armada-Hoffler development company, based in Chesapeake, Virginia, and Whitt Sessoms, a developer from Virginia Beach, submitted a site plan to the Dare County Planning Department. Sessoms's name was already familiar in Duck. His previous ventures had brought the Chevron station and the fast-food restaurant to the village. The Burger King celebrated its grand opening on September 4, 1998. Less than a year later, Crown took over the Chevron station; the pumps closed for a day in early June while workmen in ladder trucks took down one overhead sign and replaced it with another.

This time, the developers proposed a 32,000-square-foot grocery store and an adjoining 105-car parking lot. A structure that large would swallow the site they had purchased, a rise of land on the western side of Duck Road, part of the ten acres bordering the Currituck Sound, the only open space left in "downtown" Duck. The project, they promised, had already attracted the interest of a major grocery chain ready to provide a full-service store that would benefit the people of Duck.

Most residents didn't agree. By April, locals were

THIS VIEW OF "DOWNTOWN" DUCK IN THE LATE 1970s SHOWS WHAT THE
VILLAGE USED TO LOOK LIKE.
Courtesy of the Outer Banks History Center

arguing that a 1994 land-use plan protected the village from any store that wasn't small and locally owned. They took their complaints to Manteo, where county officials explained just what that 1994 land-use plan could and couldn't do. Village zoning laws prohibited neither huge franchises nor chain grocery stores. No measures had been taken to place limits on the size of businesses in the commercial area of Duck. The 1994 land-use plan, lacking the legal clout of a zoning ordinance, would be a useless defense against Armada-Hoffler, Sessoms, and the Lion. Now, it was the villagers who roared.

As June arrived, the developers claimed victory. Duck residents still hoped they could thwart the plan. Locals passed petitions; a thousand opponents signed them. Shop and restaurant owners reestablished the Duck Community Business Alliance, Ashley Copeland's husband, Mark, serving as its president and spokesperson. About the proposed Food Lion that was slated to be built directly across the street from his Roadside restaurant, Mark commented succinctly, "The people in the village just don't want it."

Duck residents were able to get a building moratorium until October for any structure exceeding ten thousand square feet, but it wouldn't impede plans for the Food Lion. The villagers had waited too long; their call to action had come too late to save the last ten acres of commercially zoned sound front. The corporate steamroller that Duck business owners like Ken Forlano heard revving its engine just outside the village limits was on its way in.

Now, all residents can do is fret—about the congestion a store this size will bring, about the already burdensome traffic that clogs the mile-long shopping district, about the safety of pedestrians and bicyclists. But the biggest worry involves sacrificing the village atmosphere, the homespun ambience that Duck's first developers fashioned almost twenty years ago. Like Ron Forlano, they know the small-town feel won't last. Some feel it slipped away the day the Burger King sign went up. Others, like natives Levin Scarborough and Ruth Tate, watched it evaporate twenty years ago, as Duck Road pushed north over the Currituck County line.

Groundbreaking for the new Food Lion store is scheduled for this fall, maybe as early as September. Perhaps Floyd will arrive first, delaying the inevitable, giving the villagers a few more days to wring their hands or prod Dare County to change its mind and turn the developers away.

With any luck, in another decade, Duck will celebrate its centennial, an official anniversary for the hundred years this Outer Banks community has had a name of its own. In the coming decade, geologists tell us, the sand beneath the village will shift more than another forty feet westward. Other hurricanes are sure to erode the beach, and other businesses are sure to squeeze into whatever space remains among the Crown, the King, and the Lion.

Wondering about the fate of their neighborhood, villagers may look to the old-timers for answers. But the old-timers already know that their Outer Banks village holds no certainties. Only change is inevitable. Wind, water, and human want all contend for the same strip of sand, each of them a fickle force that shapes this place and drives its future. Be it a rising sea or escalating development, the day is fast approaching when Duck won't seem so far from the mainland after all.

Epilogue

It starts out a dismal weekend, bleak dawns followed by hours of chilling dampness that make my teeth chatter and my joints ache. Everything in the village seems to shiver. For three days, there has been no sunshine, just a brooding sky and gales that bedevil the surf.

It is on this same weekend that a pair of ospreys glides side by side through the dank air. I first see them on a Friday, circling a section of the Currituck Sound about a mile north of the Barrier Island Station Restaurant. From a distance, they look like eagles—same majestic heads, same body size and shape, same curved bills. For a time, they sail low and close and lazy. Their white breasts almost skim the water. Then they vary the pattern of their flight, each osprey rising and dipping like a wave.

These ospreys have probably already traveled hundreds of miles. Following a route along the Atlantic shoreline, they've likely come from farther south, where they've spent most of the winter, a place that is balmy and bright, maybe the Gulf Coast or the Florida Keys.

Years ago, villagers might spot as many as two dozen ospreys nesting along the Currituck in Duck. The old-timers called the birds "fish hawks" or "fish eagles." Some still do. Duck's fishermen considered fish hawks harbingers of a good season's catch and welcomed the sight of these avian visitors in the spring and summer months.

Back then, the male birds arrived first, usually by late April, when the air warmed and mild temperatures seemed a sure thing. Spending a few carefree days cavorting like boys, the fish hawks would race one another in the skies over the Currituck. As soon as the females appeared, the sporting stopped and the courting commenced. Each male osprey would spy a mate, pursue her from behind, trail her like a shadow, gradually inching forward until he was flying alongside her. In time, she'd depend on his companionship and accept the weight of his body on her back. Together, they'd appraise the surroundings, lighting on a sound-front tree or the top of a duck blind. They'd build a nest in which to lay the fertilized eggs and wait for a family to hatch.

Today, ornithologists and ecologists value ospreys as an indicator species. These birds help gauge the general well-being of an area's ecosystem and the health of its waterways. Osprey sightings in Duck are rarer now than they were even twenty years ago. Encroaching development along the Currituck and the influx of tourists have probably chased most of the fish hawks north to Pea Island, where a bird sanctuary waits just over the county line.

Having never encountered ospreys in Duck before, I am spellbound by their grace, riveted by their excitation. I watch them swoop and climb despite a hardhearted wind that blows bitter and cuts through the trees. When a freezing rain pelts their backs, neither seems to feel it. They fly above, through, or around whatever surprises nature deals. Lifting and circling, they continue their aerial games, all the time shrieking and whistling as if lovers on holiday. They loop, then spiral, stretch their brown wings wider with each successive climb. Heaven bound, they seem to fuse into a single bird, wing tips overlapping, feathers touching.

In the 1840s, naturalist and artist John Audubon studied and drew ospreys. He seemed enamored by them, characterizing the species as demure, peace loving, and generous. Of their habits, he wrote, "The fish hawk may be said to be of a mild disposition. Not only do these birds live in perfect harmony together, but even allow birds of a very different character to approach so near as to build their nests of the very materials of which their own are constructed."

After years of examining their migration patterns and mating rituals, Audubon concluded fish hawks to be a remarkable sort, almost human in their attachment to mates and offspring and their fondness for a particular place. Ospreys will often return to the site of their birth to roost. They'll come back year after year to the same location, search out the same tree in which they built their original nest.

Neither a nature artist nor an experienced bird watcher, I find myself sharing Audubon's fascination with fish hawks. My curiosity about the ospreys grows by the hour. Late that same afternoon, despite the brutish climate and the dour sky, I come back with binoculars. I discover the ospreys not far from where I originally saw them, perched atop a ten-foot piling, a pocked and rutted wooden pole about three hundred feet from the boggy shore. It appears as if they are laying the foundation for their nest. What I see precariously balanced on that piling resembles kindling, an assortment of brittle sticks and scraps of dried wood. Perhaps this is all that remains of the nest they built the previous year.

For several hours, I watch the ospreys move from water to land and back again. They head east to the oceanfront or disappear into the woods. They return with bundles of broken branches and marsh reeds clenched in their talons. Tirelessly, they continue to gather and carry even as the wind beats water against the piling. Nightfall does not stop them.

Ospreys are creative architects and resourceful builders. All they require is a site near a waterway. They have fashioned nests on chimney and windmill tops, on utility poles and channel markers, on crags and in the roots of upturned trees. They'll scour a seaside for driftwood or a farmer's field for cornstalks. They'll collect animal bones and sheets of cardboard. While still in flight, they are capable of snapping dead branches off a pine or oak with their clawed feet. After years of repairing or remodeling the same nest, some ospreys have hefty homes weighing up to a half-ton.

On Saturday morning, I drive north on Duck Road until I reach the section of the Currituck where the ospreys worked the day before. By the time I arrive, a heavy rain has dulled to a drizzle, and the couple is already busy. The nest, barely visible to the naked eye on Friday, has grown in depth and diameter. I park the car and sit inside with my binoculars aimed at the piling. Another hard rain comes before noon, but it doesn't slow their progress. They fly off again and again, each time returning with their talons full of supplies.

With the ospreys away in the woods, I can see that the enlarged nest is sagging, probably soggy from the earlier downpours. It leans to one side, sloping over an edge of the piling. Were the wind calmer or coming from the west, the nest might not be in jeopardy. But a fierce easterly keeps prodding the ospreys' half-built home closer to peril. Helplessly, I watch it fall. It lands as gently as air, stays afloat until another howling gust stirs the water. Then it is gone.

I wait for their return. Each osprey comes back to find that its nest has vanished, its days of labor dashed in less than a minute. Neither makes any sound, no cry of despair, no screech of frustration. They merely deposit what they carry, unclenching their talons and releasing another load of materials on top of the piling. Then they fly away.

By the next afternoon, Sunday, the sun emerges. It is silver, exultant, almost blinding. My weekend in Duck nearly over, I dawdle, halfheartedly packing as the sand dries and birds chirp in the myrtles. Before leaving the village, I drive back to the Currituck and let my car idle by the side of Duck Road. I scan the sky and water for the ospreys, but I don't see them. Then I fix my focus on the top of the piling.

There, one osprey crouches motionless on a thin tuft of twigs and sea grasses, its head barely visible. Though I can see no eggs, I imagine it is the female that remains, her period of incubation already begun. The nest is partially rebuilt, the homecoming fruitful. A new generation of ospreys will soon hatch into life. Maybe two or three fledglings will be exercising their wings by the start of the tourist season. Maybe in a few years, when they mature and are ready to mate, these new ospreys will return to Duck, the place of their origin, and begin families of their own.

Above the piling, I see the other osprey circling. The expectant father flaps in the breeze, his wings spread wide, his breast broad, his cackling light as laughter.

Acknowledgments

Many magnanimous people have supported me in bringing this project to fruition. Much of the general history I have learned from the foremost historian of the Outer Banks, David Stick, who generously shared his wit and wisdom with me in person and in print. His enlightening conversation and his books *Roanoke Island: The Beginnings of English America, Dare County: A Brief History, The Outer Banks of North Carolina, The Ash Wednesday Storm*, and *An Outer Banks Reader* gave me a solid base of information and inspiration, a broad platform from which to launch my own inquiries. I am likewise indebted to science writers Judith M. Spitsbergen, Charles E. Roe, and Dirk Frankenberg for their publications on the wildlife, geology, and ecology of the Outer Banks; to historians Jeffrey Crow, Paul Escott, and Flora Hatley for *A History of African Americans in North Carolina*; and to Sarah Downing, assistant curator of the Outer Banks History Center in Manteo.

Though this manuscript centers on Duck, I found a wealth of valuable material about the village's past on the mainland of North Carolina. A heartfelt thank-you goes to Fred Fearing and Roosevelt Wright of Elizabeth City; to David Bibb and Ms. Pat Hincs at the Elizabeth City State University Library; and to the staffs at the Elizabeth City and Currituck County Public Libraries and the Museum of the Albemarle. And thanks, too, go to Mr. Brack Townsend, who spent hours on the phone with me from his home in Rocky Mount.

I would have had little to write about if it weren't for the Bias, Forlano, Copeland, and Scarborough families in Duck. And I cannot forget the dozens of Duck realtors, residents, and business owners, especially Tom Blanchard, who gave me leads or set me on the right course.

Likewise, I would like to acknowledge the work of writer Suzanne Tate, whose *Bring Me Duck* provided insights and reading pleasure.

Thanks, too, go to writers Charles Wilson, Janet Peery, and Mike Pearson for reading and critiquing this manuscript. I would also like to acknowledge North Carolina writer Philip Gerard, who encouraged me to push on until I "found the river."

For Peter and Petey, I have only love and gratitude. Without you, I would have never found my way to Duck.

Index

Advice 5 Cents, 239
Amadas, Philip, 8
Army Corps of Engineers Research Facility, 85-86, 87, 90
Audubon, John, 249-50

Barlow, Arthur, 8
Battery boxes, 167-68, 171
Beal Brothers, 223
Bender, Jay, 153, 186, 187, 188
Bias Shores, 108
Bias, John Henry, 104, 108, 111-12, 114, 116, 125, 127, 128, 144
Bias, Priscilla, 108-11, 113, 126-27
Blanchard, Tom, 208-11
Blue Point Restaurant, 4
Brimley, Herbert, 168-69
Broomstraw Rush, 5
Burgess, Major and Bethony, 30
Burgess, (Children), 30-31

Caffey, George, 6
Caffey's Inlet, 6, 58, 61, 174
Caffey's Inlet Rescue Station, 54, 55-59, 154, 158, 214-16
Cape Lookout, 6
Carova, N.C., 6

Carteret, Peter, 17-18
Catbrier, 5
Chief Okisco, 9
Coast Guard pole line, 157-58
Colleton, Sir John, 17
Commercial duck hunting, 167, 169
Copeland, Ashley, 202-8
Copeland, Mark, 204-5
Croatan Indians, 8
Currituck Banks, 6
Currituck County, N.C., 5, 8, 9
Currituck Sound, 3, 4, 6-7, 10, 18, 22-23, 24-25, 31, 63, 66, 92

Dare County, N.C., 38, 62-63, 96, 98
Dog Corner, 199
Duck blinds, 171-72
Duck Bombing and Strafing Range, 86-89
Duck General Store, 4
Duck Road, 49, 191-95, 201
Duck Waterfront Shops, 3

Evans, M. J., 203

Forlano, Ken, 226-30, 232
Forlano, Ron, 226-34, 239
Founder's Ridge, 30

Game wardens, 179
Griggs, Russell and Van, 166

Hamilton, Harry, 153, 154
Hargraves Beach, 132-34, 138-43
Hargraves, Henry, 101-8, 112-26, 127-48
Hargraves, Rosa, 103, 107, 114-21, 134-38
Hargraves Street, 102
Hariot, Thomas, 8-9
Hatteras, N.C., 9
Hines, Willie, 221-22, 224-26
Hurricanes, 128, 235-38

Jenkins, Charles, 104, 108, 114, 117-25, 127

Kellogg's Supply Company, 209-12

Lane, Ralph, 8-9

Migratory Bird Treaty Act, 167, 170

Nags Head, N.C., 27, 30, 68
North Banks, 7
North Beach Sailing, 4
North River, 8

Openauk, 8
Osprey, 248-53

Pagatour, 8
Perry, Shepard, 170-71

Perry, Walter, 153, 182-88, 189
Pine Island Gun Club, 164, 166
"Pop's" Duck Shop, 47-48
Poteskeet Indians, 7-8, 9-10, 22-23
Powder Ridge Gun Club, 161

Queen Elizabeth I, 8
Quidley, Jim, 153, 180-81

Raleigh, Sir Walter, 8, 16
Roadside Bar and Grille, 202-8
Roanoke Island, N.C., 9, 10
Rodgers family, 214, 216-20

Scarborough, Arthur, 149, 153-54
Scarborough, Daniel, 54, 59-60
Scarborough, Frank, 149-90
Scarborough, George Jr., 46-47, 51
Scarborough, George Sr., 45-46
Scarborough Lane, 43, 229
Scarborough, Levin, 35-64; family of, 43-47, 51-53, 59-60
Scarborough, Lewis, 162
Scarborough, Sue, 154-90
Sink boxes, 167-68, 171
Spanish bayonet, 5
Stick, David, 67, 68, 69-72, 77,

78-82, 85-87, 90-96

Stick, Frank, 69-72, 71, 73, 77, 90

Sunset Ice Cream, 4

Susan, Ann, 162

Tate, Ruth Scarborough, 76, 169-70, 196-202

Tate, Tommy, 82-85

Tillet brothers, 153, 173

Toler, Lloyd, 61-62

Townsend, Brack, 214-16, 220-25

Townsend, Braxton, 214, 224

Transient camps, 74-76

Weapomeiok, 9

Wee Winks, 10-12, 24

Whittie, John, 17

Wrecking, 20-22, 25, 45

Wright brothers, 69, 84-85

Utz, Blanch, 230

Yaupon, 5